Driving in Britain

A North American's guide to the ins and outs and roundabouts of driving over there

Canadian Cataloguing in Publication Data

Lockhart, Robert A. C., 1943-
  Driving in Britain

ISBN 0-9695340-0-0

1. Automobile driving - Great Britain. I. Title.

TL152.55.G7L63 1991   629.28'3'0941 C91-094528-4

691   Printed in Canada

Robert A.C. Lockhart

Driving in Britain

A North American's guide to the ins and outs and roundabouts of driving over there

Robert A.C. Lockhart

Drawings by Angry Cow

2nd Printing, June 1997

ISBN 0-9695340-0-0

Driving in Britain

A North American's guide to the ins and outs and roundabouts of driving over there

Grateful thanks to...

My dear Moira, friend and travelling companion, was the inspiration for this book in more ways than she will ever know. My thanks to her for the idea, for contributing information from Britain, and for many happy days of travel adventure.

Thanks are also due to Mother, who endured tedious hours of my silent staring at a computer screen.

My little buddy, Jason, deserves a big hug for lending me his collection of toy cars to provide visual reference for the pictures.

Many of my friends contributed their time and opinions in reviewing the manuscript. I appreciate their assistance. Special thanks to Claus for final assembly and lots of good advice.

Diolch yn fawr to Dennis Newman, for the Welsh translation on page 14.

Dan Hobbs, also known as "Angry Cow", has done a marvellous job on the drawings. They are full of whimsy and delight, exactly the qualities one should experience on a trip to Britain.

Finally, thanks to John Powell for teaching me how to drive properly, and for letting me share some of his teachings with you.

Contents

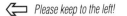

Begin reading here.

The British are known for their love of tradition. Perhaps that's why they drive on the "wrong" side of the road.

The custom originates, some say, in the very early days of sea-faring. The ancient ships were steered by a special oar or "steering board" that was always placed on the right side of the ship* and this tradition survives in the form of right-hand drive cars.

My own view is that keeping to the left really goes back to the days of King Arthur. Then, as now, most people were right-handed. So, if you were Sir Lancelot, riding a narrow trail through the enchanted forest and a strange knight approached, you would naturally keep to the left. That way, if the varlet showed any sign of hostility you would be in the best position to protect yourself using your sword in your right hand.

Whatever the true reason, the British do, in fact, drive on the opposite side of the road compared to North Americans. If you've never been to Britain before, you probably think this is <u>the</u> major difference between driving here and driving over there. It's not. Trying to remember which side of the road to drive on may be the least of your troubles. You see, driving over there is very, very different from driving at home, and it's just not clear to a

North American how British traffic really works.

For one thing, unless you're from New York, you'll find British drivers much more aggressive than you are used to. This may come as a surprise, given the media stereotype of stuffy British reserve, but really it shouldn't... after all, they didn't acquire the greatest empire the world has ever known by being a nation of wimps.

Be warned, our British cousins take their driving *very* seriously. Driving for them is A Big Deal. In North America we tend to treat the car like a washing machine... just fill it up, turn it on, and go for a spin. The British are more likely to treat the family auto like a race horse, lavishing upon it great care and attention.

Many of them drive at a very high level of skill and intensity, and all of them are very critical of others on the road. Courtesy is both expected and given, but the hesitancy of a Nervous Nellie tourist frankly gums up the works. This book aims to save you the trauma of learning by *muddling through*.

It won't tell you all the ins and outs of the British Highway Code, but it will dispel most of the confusion and help you to stay out of trouble. By doing so, I hope to keep you in touch with your original purpose for going to Britain, whether that be business or just plain old R & R.

Throughout this book, I've written from the point of view of The Driver. That's merely a convenience. If you

---

* *Hence the nautical terms "starboard", meaning the right side of a ship, and "port", meaning the left side which was always positioned against the peir so as not to damage the steering-board.*

0

Introduction

have a Travelling Companion, he or she should feel part of the team and share responsibility for navigation, at least.

If your relationship and your ego can stand it, your Travelling Companion (hereinafter known as Tee-Cee) should also be prepared to offer some knowledgeable advice such as by screaming supportively "Keep left!".

So get Tee-Cee to read this book, too, and together you can enjoy the many tiny victories that add up to a good trip. I sincerely hope this book will contribute to your enjoyment and your safety *en route*.

So, if you want to avoid nasty international incidents, and uphold the reputation of North American motorists... Read on MacDuff!

Meet the stars of this book... One of these people is "The Driver"; the other is Tee-Cee, the faithful travelling companion. Which is whom? That's up to you. In fact, the parties may switch roles freely during your trip to Britain. Oh, yes, the little English car is a star, too.... but don't count on yours looking as traditional and cute as this... more likely it will be something modern, an automotive equivalent of the type of building Prince Charles loves to hate.

1

Renting a car in Britain is not

cheap, but it is worthwhile... especially if you have a taste for adventure and enjoy the freedom of having your own wheels. But be warned... your rental car may cost more than you have been led to believe. This is explained fully in the section entitled "The Sting," but first let's look at some of the different ways you can get a car.

Being Prepared

Most tourists book a rental car in advance. That's a good thing to do, for a couple of reasons. Firstly, it's often cheaper when the car is reserved prior to leaving North America. Secondly, you can rest assured that your car will be waiting for you when you arrive.

You can book ahead two ways... do it yourself, or do it through a travel agent. Of the two, I recommend the latter. It doesn't cost any more to use an agent and your agent can recommend reliable firms offering the best combination of price and convenience to suit your individual needs. Plus, the various package deals available through an agent are often state-of-the-art when it comes to saving you money. And, should something go wong... go rong... go wrong, your travel agent has a lot of clout to make things right again.

Booking through an agent, however, usually implies paying in advance. This can be an advantage or a disadvantage, depending on whether you're a conservative or a liberal. Socialists, presumably, will be taking the bus.

Doing Your Own Thing

If self-reliant conservatism prompts you to do your own thing, you can book a car through one of the big international firms. Alternatively, track down a copy of *In Britain*, a great little magazine put out by the British Tourist Authority. You'll find it a rich source of ads for car rental firms and companies who rent *self-drive caravans* (camper vans).

In Britain can be found in many doctors' waiting rooms but if you would prefer an issue from the post-Cretaceous Period, contact the British Tourist Authority's North American subscription agent[1] (these little numbers refer you to pages 64-65, Contact People).

Being Spontaneous

If you insist, you can make your own car rental arrangements once you are across the pond... but *caveat emptor!*

You can't simply arrive at the airport and, in typical North American style, walk up to the counter of one of the familiar big international firms and demand a car. Well, you can... but they may not have one to give you, at least not the one you want. Besides, as a walk-up customer you'll likely have to pay more than you would as part of a package deal pre-booked through your travel agent.

At the airport, you may find some *car hire* (rental) firms not represented in North America that will rent you a car at a good rate but, again, you take your chances on availability.

Getting Your Wheels

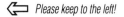 *Please keep to the left!*

Dealer's Choice

In Britain, many neigbourhood car dealers will rent you a car at a very good rate. Also, a local dealer might be particularly convenient if you are being met by friends at the airport and you plan to stay with them awhile before venturing off on your own.

Your British friends can tell you which dealers offer rentals and they can check out the prices for you.

One factor to consider is that a local car dealer won't have a nation-wide network of depots. You may get all the way to Land's End before your cute little car reveals that its true colours are lemon yellow and, unlike the big firms, there will be no local office to give you lemon-aid.

So make sure the dealer belongs to the AA (Automobile Association) or the RAC (the Royal Automobile Club). You'll see their little service vehicles buzzing about everywhere in Britain. The auto clubs will look after you even if the dealer can't.

Half-a-league, half-a-league, half-a-league on...

Some firms allow unlimited mileage for no extra charge and some don't. Those that charge by the mile usually offer a lower daily rate and a modest number of "free" miles. If you're on a carefully planned itinerary, a deal like this might save you money.

If your plans are loose, though, you don't want the miles clicking off like a Chinese water torture... go for the deal with unlimited mileage. You may think you can't travel far in a little country like Britain, but I once rolled up almost 2,000 miles in ten days just visiting relatives within a 100-mile radius of Glasgow.

Another thing to watch out for is drop-off charges. If you plan to enter and leave Britain via the same airport, there's no problem... you'll be returning the car to where you got it. If, however, you plan to arrive at London and leave via Prestwick, make sure you can drop off the car without having to pay extra.

Cheap Shot

The cheapest option, of course, is to borrow a car from family or friends. But, please, do not ever *ask* to borrow a car! Wait until it is offered. There are societies where they will lend you a wife with less trepidation than the British suffer in lending you a car.

However, if it's your good fortune to be held in such high regard by your British allies that you are offered the loan of a car, consider first the strain that a *bashed wing* (dented fender) may place on your friendship. At the very least, ask your friends to check with their insurance agent and offer to pay any extra premium.

And don't forget to return your borrowed car full of *petrol*. Fuel in Britain costs two or three times the price we pay in North America and returning a car empty will earn you the same social disdain afforded those who fail to buy a round at the local pub.

Collision Damage Wager

Many first-time travellers are shocked and annoyed to discover something called the "Collision Damage Waiver". This confusingly-named, and outrageously-priced, charge can knock big holes in your budget if it catches you by surprise. Here's what it's about...

If you crunch your hired car in a *roundabout* (traffic circle), <u>someone</u> has to pay. Typically, in Britain, the car hire firm's insurance will only cover damage in excess of the first £250-400. That means that YOU, the driver, will be responsible for this amount... unless you buy the Collision Damage Waiver.

Buying this extra protection will cost £3 to £5 per day plus the 17.5% *Value Added Tax* (British baffleblab for "sales tax" a.k.a. "GST"). If you buy the Collision Damage Waiver, you can crunch the car with financial impunity... though you cannot escape the moral and legal responsibility to avoid damaging the car as best you can.

In fact, if it can be shown that you were breaking the law at the time of the crunch, the Collision Damage Waiver can be disallowed. In practice, however, the rental firms and the insurers tend to be somewhat forgiving of honest mistakes.

So, even if you pre-paid your car rental before leaving home, be prepared to pay several pounds per day once you get there. Granted, the Collision Damage Waiver is optional. You don't *have* to pay it, but consider the nightmare potential of NOT being protected...

Working Without a Net

If you habitually enjoy the impossible good luck of Indiana Jones, you may decide to gamble and reject the Collision Damage Waiver. Okay, but you are liable for any damage to the car, no matter how caused, up to a typical maximum of about $600. Thus if an errant ewe leaps over a *stane dyke* (stone wall) and *bashes your bonnet* (dents the hood), you must cough up enough coin of the realm to have it *sorted* (fixed) and *resprayed* (painted).

Also, just because you decide to throw prudence to the winds and refuse the Collision Damage Waiver, don't expect the car hire firm to share your gamble. They are understandably averse to draughts on their financial nether regions and they will cover their buns with your money. This is done with quiet discretion when they ask for an impression from your credit or charge card. That impression, with your signature on it, is a like a blank cheque for them to fill in as necessary.

Even unsigned, your card impression is effectively a blank cheque because you WILL certainly be asked to sign a rental agreement. With your signature thus "on record" the company can process charges against your account... even after you are long gone. In my experience, car rental firms can be trusted to do the decent thing and process only legitimate charges. This makes it possible in a pinch to simply toss the car keys to a desk clerk as you sprint past the counter in a desperate attempt to catch your plane home.

The $ting

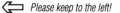 *Please keep to the left!*

Personal Injury & Liability

Many companies offer personal injury insurance for a small daily charge. But, you should have already purchased personal health insurance for your trip and you won't need double coverage.

As regards your liability for running over some unfortunate Briton, you may already be covered by your auto insurance policy at home. But don't assume anything. Call your agent and find out exactly what your rights are.

The Bottom Line

These extra charges are a nuisance and perhaps even a rip-off since the pro-rated annual rate is several hundred percent more than you pay for similar coverage on your own car, but it's not worth taking a chance with your holiday so hold your nose and pay up.

Diogenes' Choice

If you find this stuff confusing and all you really want to know is "How can I get a good car, and what will it cost?" then you have another option.

In defiance of long-standing commercial tradition, a few brave firms now have the gumption to advertise their actual bottom-line package price including collision damage waiver, all taxes, insurance, and unlimited mileage. There are no hidden extras, no surprises. What-you-see-is-what-you-get. Though the price may *look* higher, in reality, it is likely to be competive. If you value honesty in advertising, seek out these champions of truth.②

It's a Plastic World

Whatever your views on the merits and morality of plastic money, renting a car overseas without a major card is very difficult, and requires more cash than an Arab shiekh on a shopping spree at Harrod's with multiple wives. Without major plastic, rental firms are leery of doing business with you, and you may be asked to plunk down the full amount of the collision deductible IN CASH! This will be refunded if you return the car undamaged but your holiday budget will be shot.

Cards which automatically insure you when used to rent a car (Amex is prominent amongst these) give you an option... you don't *have* to buy the hateful Collision Damage Waiver... though you may *wish* to. Here's why:

- A hefty security deposit may be charged to your card (nicked me for £1500 once). Though it's refunded if you return the car unscathed, any costs incurred by misadventure will be charged to your account until the claim is processed by the card company's insurance agency.

- If your car is stolen or damaged you will have to cope with correspondence, phone calls and hassles relating to the claim. Plus you are liable for a deductible, typically $100. But if you bought the CDW you can just shrug and walk away smiling.

My bottom-line advice? Use a major card, *and* buy the CWD. It's less hassle and you'll sleep better.

How Much Car?

Having decided how, when, and from whom you are going to get a car, you must now decide what kind of car to get. Whatever you choose, you're in for a treat because even the smallest and cheapest British car will probably seem exotic to you. Even the familiar brand names will be different because they'll be European specification and generally they handle better and go faster than the same marques at home.

The cheapest cars to rent are, naturally, the smallest. A little economy car with a 1100 cc engine is a typical 'A' Category offering. If there are only two of you and you don't pack like rock stars on tour, the A-car will be a blast. If puddle-jumpers aren't your style, you may need or want something bigger. No problem, you'll just have to pay more (see below).

Getting The Gears

Except for the luxury class, you should know that most British cars have a stick shift. You can pay extra to get an automatic but, often, you won't be very happy with it... little cars with automatics are about as satisfying as sharing a hot-tub with Dolly Parton and having your glasses fog up.*

So, if you want to keep up with the traffic, handle steep grades without embarrassment, and generally feel good about your driving overseas, opt for a manual shift car. If you normally drive an automatic, maybe you should borrow your neighbour's Rabbit to practice shifting before you go abroad.

However, if shifting gears is beneath your personal dignity or truly beyond your ken, then perhaps you should book an automatic after all. If you do, be sure the car has an engine at least as big as 1300 cc. Anything smaller is not only joyless, but (I think) dangerously underpowered.

You'll pay twice over for your shiftlessness... once for the automatic transmission, once again for the bigger car.

Getting Lucky

If your travelling companion, spouse, or whatever is always last off the plane, last through Immigration, and seems to stop at *the loo* (toilet) at every opportunity, you should be grateful.

Why? Because there is a very good chance that everyone else on the plane will have picked up their rental car by the time you finally belly up to the counter. There's also a good chance that all of the A-cars on hand have been signed out.

If you have a pre-booked reservation, the company will have to give you a bigger and better car, perhaps even an exotic new Sierra or a comfy Cavalier, FOR THE SAME PRICE! It's one of the few occasions when there really is a free lunch.

---

* *My editors have criticised this remark as transparently male in origin and appeal. I maintain, however, that anyone in the circumstance described would be consumed by natural curiosity and therefore would be frustrated by such inopportune fogging of the ocular appliances.*

Kicking the Tyres

⇐ Please keep to the left!

Free Lessons

If you are flying to London and plan to spend a few days seeing the sights, don't rent a car at all... at least not at first. For tourists in London, a car is just an expensive nuisance. So, take *The Tube* (subway), ride the double-deckers, walk, and (best of all) take taxis. You get a special bonus from the taxi drivers... unlike the hosers we too often get at home, British cabbies are top-notch professional drivers. In fact, London cabbies have to study for three years and pass rigorous exams to earn their licence! So watch what they do, ask them questions, and generally relax and have a good time while you get free lessons on driving in Britain.

Then, when the British Museum has lost its charm and you are ready to fly solo, pick up your pre-booked rental car (about 10:00 a.m., after rush hour) and blow town. Better still, ask the car hire firm to deliver your car to your hotel... many will do so cheerfully.

Merely an appliance?

To some, the automobile is just a utilitarian device, something to get one from A to B. For others, the auto is an emotional machine... an extension of the psyche, an expression of lifestyle and philosophy. In the same way, for some, touring Britain isn't just a holiday, it's a happening — a chance to live out fantasies of green hills and laughing fields of golden daffodils... stately homes and village inns... the rich smell of leather and the feel of burled walnut.

If you know what I'm talking about, you may want something special to complete your British experience. Consider these possibilities.

Licensed To Thrill

If you share James Bond's taste for beautiful women, Dom Pérignon, and exotic cars, the latter can be obtained from Avis and a few other firms.③ If you are stirred by fine cars, and not shaken by the price, you can drive a Rolls Royce, Jaguar, Porsche, Ferrari... you name it. Of course, you'll pay dearly for your discerning tastes, but if it's worth it to you, it's good value. Right?

Some of Avis' best customers, by the way, are film-makers who need a bit of flash and a touch of class to spice up their tale. Keep a sharp lookout, you might see "your" car on *telly*.

Something Special

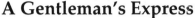
A Gentleman's Express

Just picture yourself... doodling through the dales of Yorkshire in a rag-top Morgan... cruising the Cotswolds in a zippy MG. If these are part of your fantasy, you or your travel agent should contact a firm called Sports Car Hire.④ For an appropriate (but not outrageous) extra fee, they will put you behind the wheel of a classic British sports car.

À la Belle Époque

If you really want to do things in style, you can arrange to see Britain from the back seat of a distinguished automobile. Several firms[5] supply chauffeur-driven cars for whatever period you require, even if it's just a night out at the theatre. On request, you can even get nice little extras such as picnic hampers and a chilled bottle of hock. There are also special rates for those attending Royal Garden Parties and Investitures.

Once, while travelling with a film crew assigned to a minister of the Crown, I had occasion to be met by a uniformed chauffeur at Heathrow Airport (my importance had been wildly misconstrued!). The *wee chappie* (dutiful servant) haughtily disdained our offers of assistance as he loaded all of our personal baggage and bulky film equipment onto a trolley. Then he led us briskly through the teeming cosmopolitan throng, bellowing out the stentorian command:
"MAKE WAY FOR NAVAL OFFICER!
 MAKE WAY FOR NAVAL OFFICER!"

In his smart blue uniform and peaked cap, our chauffeur looked more like an officer than we did in our denims, but nevertheless the crowd parted before us like the Red Sea before Moses. How he ever got all those bulky camera cases and bags into the *boot* (trunk) of a Rolls I'll never know. What a way to go!

Wheels of Fortune

⇐ Please keep to the left!

A Swede-heart of a Deal

Are you tired of your Mercedes because they're so common? Weary of the Teutonic intensity of your BMW? Or, perhaps you need a sporty alternative to spare your Cadillac the indignity of competing in the country club's annual gumball rally?

Well, cheer up because there's a refreshing automotive antidote... how about buying a spiffy new car as part of your holiday overseas?

You can order a brand new, North American spec, Volvo or Saab for delivery overseas and you can save pots of money... perhaps enough to pay for your airfare and for shipping the car back home and paying duty. You also enjoy "free" wheels for the duration of your stay in Britain (they lend you a right-hand drive car).

Exactly how the Swedes got into the act is beyond me, but check it out.⑥

Your licence, please.

Contrary to popular belief, you don't need an International Driver's Licence in Britain. The licence you use at home will do nicely — remember to bring it.

You must produce a valid licence before you can rent a car, it must have been valid for the past 12 months, and it must show that you are old enough to be trusted (21-25 years, depending on the company), and not too old to be insured (usually 70 years of age).

Keep your licence and the car rental agreement with you all the time you are driving in case you neglect to read the rest of this book and therefore attract the scrutiny of a bobby.

Also, if more than one person is going to drive, say so. The second person will also have to sign up.

Fuellish Advice

One more thing... before you drag your baggage and your drooping body out to the *car park* (parking lot), ask the rental people what kind of fuel your car uses.

Fuels in Britain are sold by octane rating and small cars typically take *3-star* fuel. But unleaded *petrol* (dispensed from vivid green hoses) is now very popular so find out for certain what your car drinks and write it on the rental agreement envelope for handy reference when it comes time to enter your first *filling station*.

The Vehicle Check

Before you get into your rental car, do a circle check... walk slowly around the vehicle looking for dents, scratches, broken lights and flat or bulging *tyres*. Usually, the car will be in perfect shape but if you do find a fault, report it to the rental company immediately. That way, they can't blame you.

If you're really keen, look under the *bonnet* (hood) as well. Check the oil, and look for bulging hoses and loose belts. Keep an eye peeled for the unexpected. I once discovered a cute little kitten in the engine compartment. It had apparently crawled in to snuggle up to the warm engine. Another time I found a ball-peen hammer. I'm still trying to figure out what possible application such an instrument could have in the proper maintenance of a BMW.

Anyway, if everything's cool, then load your luggage into the *boot* (trunk), being especially careful to safely wedge your duty-free booze against the potentially abrupt manoeuvres of your first exciting encounter with British traffic.

The Driver should now get into the car (right side, please) and have Tee-Cee or an innocent passer-by confirm that brake lights, turn signals, headlights, etc. work. (That funny red light hanging down from the rear bumper has nothing to do with the profession of the previous tenant. It's a special, high-intensity fog light for use in case you are lucky enough to encounter a traditional British fog festival.)

Afore ye go...

The Cockpit Drill

You're in a strange car, you feel like everything is backwards and, you've probably been awake all night. Thus disadvantaged, you're about to face hectic airport traffic in a bewildering foreign environment. Under these conditions, do you really want to try and find the horn, adjust the mirrors, and shift the seat as you drive out of the airport? Of course not, you do all that before you even start.

Take time to look around the cockpit and learn where all of the controls are and how they work. Tee-Cee won't be very impressed if you try to signal turns by washing the *windscreen*.

Once you've learned what every switch, lever, button and twiddle on the *fascia* (dashboard) does, adjust the seat for some sportsmanlike driving (see Appendix, Advanced Driving).

Now that you're properly seated, adjust the mirrors, do up your seat belt (compulsory) and start the car. The car will almost certainly have a manual choke. Pull it out to start, remember to turn it off as soon as the motor will run smoothly without it.

Moving Out

With the engine running, go through the gears. It'll feel a bit awkward using your left hand, and you may accidently downshift Tee-Cee's right kneecap, but you'll probably find your favourite gears right where you expect them. Don't forget reverse... you may have to push down, pull up, or otherwise prod the gearshift in some unconventional manner to persuade it into reverse. It will be better for your blood pressure if you learn to do this here in the *car park*, rather than on the *high street* (main drag) with a humungous *lorry* (Mack truck) *hooting* at you.

Left is Right

Okay, presuming that you've checked a map and know where you're headed, or better still, that you've designated Tee-Cee to be chief navigator and thus have someone to blame for all wrong turns, you are ready to roll. Remember, keep left! Try this little trick to keep oriented... *Keep the centreline of the roadway next to the steering wheel.* That's it's proper position at home or abroad so it's easy to remember.

That sign? Oh, it says,
"Welcome to Wales... Keep Wales tidy,
dump your rubbish in England."

Signs of Progress

⟸ *Please keep to the left!*

Signs, by their very nature, ought to be fairly self-explanatory. But there are several different types of signs used in Britain and you should know what to expect. Here are some general guidelines…

Round signs give orders…

Left Turn
FORBIDDEN

Right Turn
FORBIDDEN

Parking
FORBIDDEN

Entry
FORBIDDEN

YOU MUST
Turn Left

YOU MUST
Turn Right

YOU MUST
Go Straight-on

YOU MUST
Keep Left or Right
(Pick one!)

Triangular signs give warnings…

WARNING!
Change to opposite
carriageway.

WARNING!
Dual carriageway ends.

WARNING!
Road works ahead.

*(This signs always makes
me think of politicians.)*

Direction signs

These usually indicate towns, rather than compass direction. This system is based on the assumption that anyone smart enough to drive must surely have a comprehensive knowledge of British geography.

If some ghastly oversight in your education has failed to instruct you that Chipping Sodbury is somewhat south of Wooton-Under-Edge, don't worry... just learn where a few of the big cities are with reference to London and you'll do reasonably well.

With regard to direction signs...

◀▫ Blue signs shaped like this pertain to *motorways* (freeways), which are always designated M-something.

◀▫ Dark green signs pertain to, and they are found on, primary roads (which are always designated A-something).

With typical British penchant for understatement, when towns or roads are given in *parentheses* (the A44, Broadway, in this example), what they mean to say is this: *In this direction but not exactly on this road. Go this way but watch for your turn-off (the A44) further along.*

◀▫ This sign says you are on the A46, Lincoln is 12 miles ahead, Sherwood is 28 miles. Nottingham is not on the A46, but it's in this direction 43 miles away. Distances are in miles, but this may change with increasing EEC integration.

Signs of Progress

Alternatively, foist the entire burden of pathfinding on Tee-Cee and follow Tee-Cee's instructions instantly and without question. If, however, you are a chronic Doubting Thomas, pull off to the side of the road to discuss the situation. Always do this in front of a sign so that your discussions can have a factual, rather than a merely speculative or recriminatory basis. You'll find that the British have thoughtfully provided confirmatory distance and destination signs just beyond every major intersection.

For more tips on finding your way, see the section on Pathfinding.

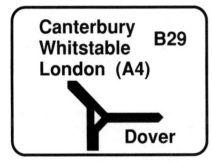

⬅ıııı Black & white signs pertain to secondary roads (which are always B-something). In the case shown here, if you follow the B29 to Canterbury and Whitstable, you'll eventually reach the A4 which, in turn, leads you to London.

Note: There are also C-roads, which tend to be very narrow.

⬅ıııı Blue borders indicate local features such as car parks and public loos.

⬅ıııı These are the signs you travel to Britain for. They point to castles, stately homes, follies, palaces, etc. There are quite a variety of styles, some blue, some brown, but whatever their appearance, they almost certainly lead to history and adventure.

17

Lifelines

One of the first things you'll notice driving out of the airport is that road signs in Britain look different. But here's something you <u>won't</u> notice... THE WHITE LINES PAINTED ON THE ROAD ARE JUST AS IMPORTANT AS THE SIGNS!

Also essential to your safety are the invisible rules of right-of-way by which the Brits derive order out of seeming chaos. Please read this section several times and study the diagrams carefully. *This information is crucial!*

The Right to Rule

The general rule in Britain is: *Give way to traffic coming from your right.*

This principle also applies in North America but we don't get much practice because our traffic engineers don't really trust us to manage without signs and signals. By contrast, in lightly-travelled areas of Britain, including especially *housing estates* (subdivisions), there are many uncontrolled *junctions* protected only by a confident belief

that everyone understands yield-to-the-right. Like most rules in a class-conscious society, however, there are exceptions based on your status... not your ancestry whether you are on the most important road. If you are, and especially if you see one of these signs as you approach a junction, it's probably safe to assume you have right-of-way over small lanes entering from the right. But, watch out for (gasp!) the deadly Painted Rattlesnakes.

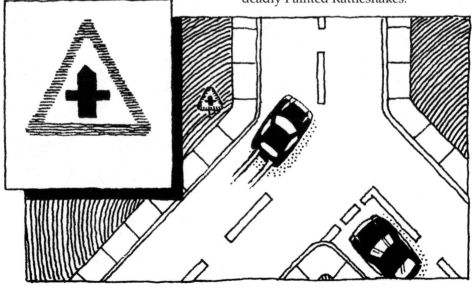

Painted Rattlesnakes

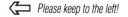

The Deadly Dash

A broken or dashed white line painted across your part of the road is like a sleeping rattlesnake waiting for you to step on it! These Deadly Dashes lurk mostly at intersections where they indicate that YOU must now *Give Way* (yield) at this point.

To the British this is perfectly clear, but painted lines seem insignificant to North Americans accustomed to big signs and flashing lights. That's what makes these dashed white sidewinders so deadly... they are easy to overlook, but loaded with danger. Treat them as you would a "Yield" sign back home.

The Double Deadly Dash

The dashed white *Give Way* marking comes in two varieties, Deadly and Double Deadly. The distinction in law between the two may animate the interest of Rumpole of the Bailey but, for the tourist, both varieties of painted rattlesnake mean exactly the same thing... DO NOT CROSS THIS LINE UNLESS THE WAY IS CLEAR!

Watch out for Deadly Dashes even on major roads where they can be encountered suddenly and without warning. There may or may not be a sign at the intersection, but you must *Give Way* anyhow. Similarly, there may or may not be a warning triangle painted on the roadway.

The Deadly Dash
A single dashed white line across your path means: "Give Way"

The Double Deadly Dash
A double dashed white line across your path means: "Give Way or else!"

A particularly venomous

variety of Deadly Dash lurks at oblique intersections (see illustrations). As you approach the Y-junction, you see an open road ahead and, unless you're wary, you may drive right across the Deadly Dash into a stream of high-speed merging traffic. Often, there will be no provision for merging except the expectation that a bit of dashed white paint will prompt you to play "After you, Alphonse!"

   Please note, you are not necessarily required to actually STOP for Deadly Dashes... just slow down and check traffic before you enter the intersection. Remember to do this and you'll be okay... forget, and your heart will be pumping in overdrive.

The White-Striper

This variety of painted rattlesnake is not so sneaky as the Deadly Dash variety because you are already familiar with its habits.

   At stop signs and traffic lights there is always a solid white line indicating where you should stop. Usually, there is also a STOP sign or a red light to reinforce the message. All of this is no surprise, it works just that way at home. Just don't try to turn on a red light. Woody Allen once said, "Being allowed to turn on a red light is one of the few cultural benefits of living in California." Maybe so, but don't do it in Britain without a green filter light.

The Driver's Point of View
The driver anticipates the main intersection farther ahead, but watch out for the Deadly Dash nearby!

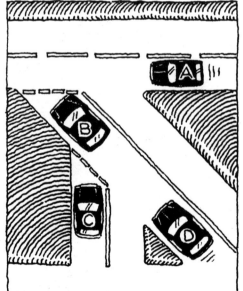

The Foul Creature Revealed!
An overhead view reveals details of a Painted Rattlesnake ambush.

Who must Give Way to whom?

B gives way to A;
C gives way to D.

Painted Rattlesnakes

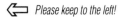 *Please keep to the left!*

Box Junctions

Occasionally, you'll encounter a junction totally criss-crossed with yellow lines rather like a fisherman's net. The message here is the same as it would be for Charlie the Tuna... Don't get caught!

In other words, don't enter this *box junction* unless your exit is clear. If traffic gets blocked and leaves you stranded on the yellow lines, you'll probably get vigourously *hooted* at, you'll certainly get frustrated, and you could be fined.

By the way, similar criss-cross markings are found at railway crossings where, presumably, you need little encouragement not to proceed onto the tracks unless you have a clear exit.

The drawing below shows what NOT to do.

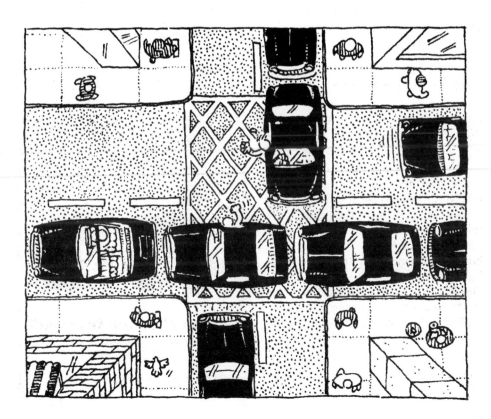

Zebra Crossings

Oh, yes... there is a peculiar sub-species of Deadly Dash found lurking only at *Zebra Crossings*. Whether or not you visit a *safari park* (game farm), you're going to encounter many of these Zebra Crossings.

Strangely, they are most often found in towns, where they are frequently exploited by human beings attempting to cross the street. The Zebra Crossing variety of painted rattlesnake is easily recognised by their distinctive black and white markings (see picture) and they are often accompanied by flashing amber lights known as *Belisha Beacons.**

---

* *So-named after Lord Hore-Belisha, Minister of Transport in 1934 when the flashing lights were introduced... a useful bit of trivia to impress the denizens of your favourite "local" (pub).*

The rule at Zebra Crossings is this... STOP IF A PEDESTRIAN IS STANDING ON THE CROSSING.

That's why a Deadly Dash is always painted on the roadway in front of a Zebra Crossing... YOU, the driver, must Give Way to pedestrians who are actually on the crossing. If they are still on the *pavement* (the sidewalk) but they are casting puppy dog looks of entreaty in your direction, let conscience be your guide. Keep in mind, however, that the motorists behind you may be surprised by unexpected generosity to pedestrians.

Painted Rattlesnakes

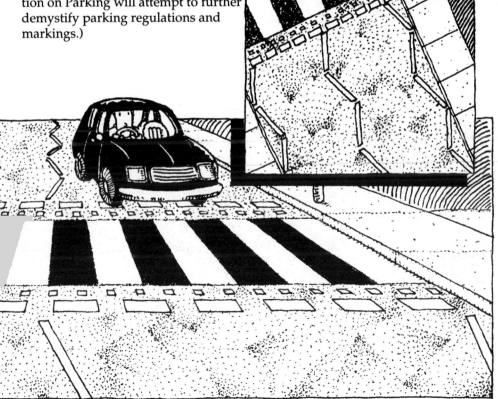

⇐ *Please keep to the left!*

Zig-zags

In the drawings, you'll notice that the lane markings near Zebra Crossings go a little wonky. They're trying to tell you something...

- "Warning, there's a Zebra Crossing ahead!"
- "No passing from here to crossing"
- "No waiting or parking here!"

Yellow zig-zags painted along the *kerb* have nothing to do with zebras, they exist to tell you that any parking or unnecessary stopping at this point will be frowned upon. (The next section on Parking will attempt to further demystify parking regulations and markings.)

Pelican Crossings

A pedestrian crossing controlled by a push-button traffic light is called a *Pelican Crossing*. I don't know why. Your response to Pelican Crossings is easy...

- If the light is red, STOP.
- If the light is green, GO.
- If the light is flashing amber, Give Way to any pedestrians (or pelicans) who happen to be on the crossing.

If no-one is on the crossing, you may proceed with caution on the flashing amber.

The Waiting game

By North American standards, parking policies in Britain (and in Europe generally) are downright permissive. For the most part, parking space is pretty well catch-as-catch-can. This is not to suggest, however, that there are no rules. There are, and they are enforced.

The various and sundry *Waiting Restrictions* (parking regulations) are communicated to the citizenry through the combined media of baffling signs and a distinctive species of painted rattlesnake that takes the form of yellow lines painted along the *kerb*.

A single yellow line along the kerb means "RESTRICTED PARKING". In other words, sometimes you can, sometimes you can't. Details may be found on signs afixed to nearby posts.

A double yellow line means "NO WAITING". Not only can you not park here, you can't even pause to let passengers *alight* (get off or on).

Yellow zig-zag lines convey the message, "DON'T EVEN THINK OF PARKING HERE!"

Together, these lines and signs comprise an elaborate code devised, I speculate, by an ex-Bletchley cryptographer. Frankly, they are beyond my ken. If they seem simple here it's only because I've addressed just what my feeble comprehension can encompass.

If you are a fan of Big Blue computers and thus love to crack arcane codes, I invite you to delve into the British *Highway Code* ⑦ and examine the regulations in their full richness. If, like me, you prefer not to clutter your brain with weird ciphers then do what I do when I'm in Britain — just stay away from little yellow varmints!

I've told you the most important of the yellow line codes and provided a sampler of typical signs. Apart from these basic regulations, let common sense and conscience be your guide.

Should these latter guides prove untrustworthy, don't worry about how you're going to pay for your parking tickets. Your sins will seek you out...

Sin Tax Error

In Britain they're called *Traffic Wardens*. You may know them as Traffic Control Officers... Meter Maids... Green Hornets... or other terms too colourful and expressive to print here.

You may think you can avoid their sting by simply tearing up the ticket and escaping to Sacramento or Saskatoon. Maybe you'll escape scot-free; maybe you won't. Tickets will be added to your car rental bill if they come through in time. If not, you might still get a letter containing a demand for payment.

The decent thing to do is confess your sins when you turn in the car.

Parking

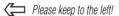 *Please keep to the left!*

NO STOPPING

This sign, or variations thereof, indicates an *urban clearway*, no parking, no stopping to let folk in or out, no waiting… in other words, keep moving!

NO WAITING

This sign, or variations thereof (see examples below), indicates you can stop to let Tee-Cee *alight*, but you can't wait while Tee-Cee washes your *knickers* at the local laundramat.

At any time

Mon - Fri
7:30 am - 6:00 pm

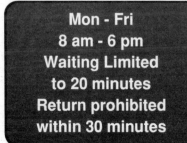

**Mon - Fri
8 am - 6 pm
Waiting Limited
to 20 minutes
Return prohibited
within 30 minutes**

URBAN CLEARWAY
Monday to Friday

am 8-9:30	pm 4:30-6:00

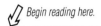

Round'n'Round She Goes

Outside the Scottish town of East Kilbride there is an intersection called the "Whirlies Roundabout". Never was a place more descriptively named.

I defy any tourist lacking nerves of steel and a map of Western Scotland inscribed on the inside of the cranium to negotiate this whirling dervish, this *mælström* of motordom, and survive the experience with tranquility intact and sense of direction not screaming TILT!

And yet, the Whirlies is not really unusual... it is a thoroughly typical British *roundabout* (known to North Americans who remember them, as a traffic circle). You'll find roundabouts everywhere you go in Britain.

The British love them because they keep everyone moving and thus save lots of time, frustration and energy. Apart from these very practical considerations, I speculate there is a much deeper cultural significance...

Look closely at Stonehenge. Do you think that circular shape is just coincidence? Hah!

And what about those mysterious phenomena known as *crop circles*? Inexplicable, perfect, *circular* shapes that appear in healthy field crops overnight. They look for all the world as if flying saucers had rested there, crushing the crops... but the stems of corn or wheat are never broken, just gently bent by some mysterious *circular* force!

Roundabouts

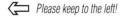

I could go on and on… *round* barrows, ancient burial sites… Avebury Circle, bigger than Stonehenge… mammoth, man-made Silbury Hill where, even today, modern witches still sometimes dance naked at midnight around the *circular* hilltop…

Are roundabouts a manifestation of ancient mystical forces latent in the British psyche? I don't know, but while Britons embrace them with characteristic enthusiasm; they can be terrifying for the poor, bemused tourist from grid-oriented North America. They are certainly the biggest single challenge facing the tourist driver.

So, tune in to the ancient mystic power of circles. Read how roundabouts work, discover how you can learn to make them work for you. And, as you enter the magic circles for the first time…

May The Force be with you!

Know thine enemy

Here it is, the principal pall cast over your equanimity while driving in Britain... a typical, garden-variety roundabout. Notice particularly the sequence and types of signs.

1 The first warning of a roundabout ahead is a dark green direction sign with a characteristic wagon-wheel shape. In addition to showing which *main* roads are coming up, the big direction sign is your main chance to figure out where you are going (which town to head for) and which road to take.

   Depending on the acuity of your vision, your speed, and the percipience of your navigator (good ol' Tee-Cee!), you'll have about three blinks of a flirt's eye to absorb all this information and make your decision. The chapter on Pathfinding gives tricks for doing this.

2 On some roundabouts you will encounter a second, black & white direction sign. This is for local destinations only... the Piddling Parsonbys of Britain, not the major cities.

3 As you approach the jaws of the roundabout, notice the official roundabout warning symbol residing inside an official triangular warning sign. Do some serious slowing down at this point.

4 There is a Deadly Dash at the entrance to every roundabout. That means you must GIVE WAY to any traffic already on the roundabout. Look right, turn left!

5 Last-minute warning is provided by chevrons pointing to the left (you always turn *left* at roundabouts!).

6 Each exit is marked by pointed signs. Dark green ones point to major centres, black & white ones point to local places. Blue & white signs indicate things such as castles, cathedrals and public *loos*.

7 After each exit, there is (almost) always a confirmatory destination sign to reassure you that you're on the right road. This sign will also tell you how far it is to the various places that lie ahead down this road.

Note... Small, round signs resembling the hood ornament on a turbo-charged hatchback warn that you are about to enter a mini-roundabout. The arrows always go clockwise; so should you.

A Typical Roundabout

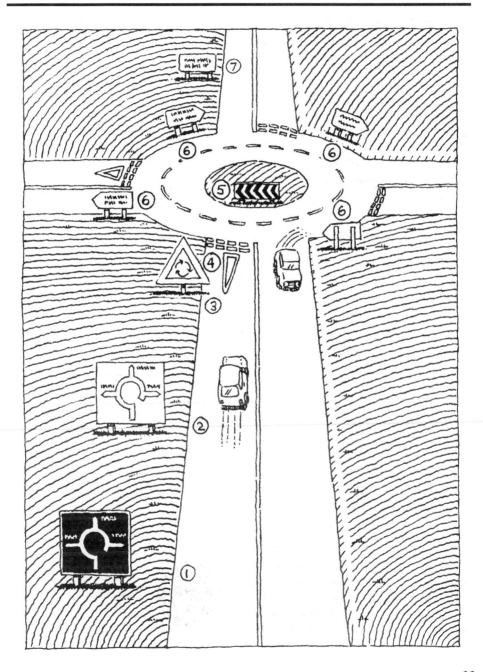

Mind Games

In North America, traffic control seems based on inertia. By contrast, the British system is based on momentum. Thus, the purpose of the roundabout is to keep traffic moving. It's important for you, the tourist, to remember that... keep moving!

If you let fear or indecision slow you down, you'll *cause* trouble and you'll *have* trouble with roundabouts. Be cautious, but don't be timid.

Roundabouting is a complex endeavour so try to *imagine* your way through the roundabouts... Mentally

1/ Give way to traffic

Each entry point is marked by a Deadly Dash. Thus, YOU, the entering motorist, must Give Way to the right. Besides, traffic on the roundabout always has *priority* (right-of-way) over entering traffic.

So, slow down, stop if you must, but do not enter the roundabout until it can be done without upsetting anyone already in the circle.

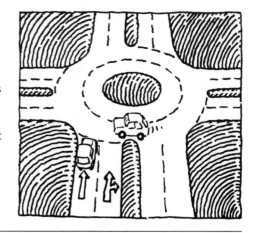

2/ Turning left

When turning left, keep left all the way through the roundabout. Use the Outer Circle only.

You should have your left turn signal on from before the Deadly Dash until you exit.

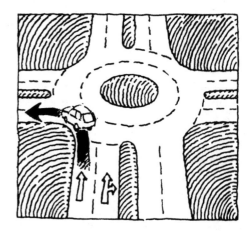

The Simple Roundabout

project yourself into the drawings and, one lesson at a time, try to picture what is happening.

Study the drawings very carefully. They show the simplest form of roundabout... if you understand how this works the more elaborate ones will be duck soup.

More Right-Thinking

As you know, the general rule in Britain is "Give way to the right!" This also applies <u>within</u> the roundabout. Thus, if someone wishes to cross in front of you from the Inner Circle to the Outer Circle or to an exit, let them do it... they have the right!

3/ Going "straight on"

When going *straight on*, the best technique is to approach using the left-most lane and plan to use the Outer Circle of the roundabout.

It is quite proper and legal to use the Inner Circle, but it's not the easiest approach for neophytes.

Begin your turn signal when your exit is the next one coming up.

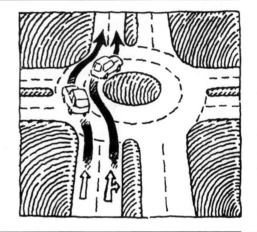

4/ Going to the right

When going to the right, or taking any exit past 12 o'clock, approach in the right-most lane (if you have a choice). When the coast is clear, move into the Inner Circle and hug the round grassy bit. When your exit is next up, begin to signal then go straight out.

As you exit, you must cross the Outer Circle again... this is the danger point! Although you have the right-of-way, watch out for cars that have just entered or speed-crazed zoomers trying to pass you on the inside.

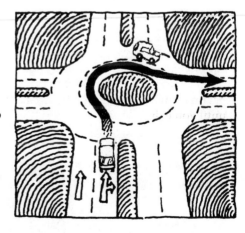

Begin reading here.

The Circle of Doom

If you tried the cerebral circumnavigation I urged upon you overleaf, you now realize that the further you go around a roundabout, the harder it gets. But just in case your imaginary images are still a bit too rosy, let me tell you what it's really like in the Circle of Doom...

• *You are proceeding briskly around the Inner Circle of a large roundabout. It's a rather tight turn, and you're pulling hard on the wheel as you look anxiously ahead for a turn-off sign that bears a name you recognise. Silently, you are thankful for the seat belt holding you firmly in place against the insistent tug of centrifugal force. (Funny, Tee-Cee's never make that peculiar screeching noise before... or maybe it's just the tyres??)*

Stay in the Outer Circle all the way around — As a social misdemeanor this falls midway between B.O. and halitosis... but, darn it, it works! It simplifies your driving task by saving you the trauma of changing lanes in the midst of aggressive traffic.

The chief hazard of staying in the Outer Circle all the way around is that someone who is *entering* might think you are about to *exit* and therefore nip out in front of you. To avoid such unpleasant misunderstandings, *pul-leese* make sure your turn signal is OFF until just before your exit. Otherwise, you may get to exploit that very expensive Collision Damage Waiver you purchased so reluctantly.

Roundabout Tactics

⇐ *Please keep to the left!*

- *Meanwhile, cars are rocketing all around you... entering, exiting, crossing from lane to lane, and maybe even passing you on the inside. Coping with all of this pressure as best you can, this is what you must do...*

- *Your turn-off is the next exit, so check your wing mirror, signal, shoulder check, and mentally cross your fingers. NOW! dash from the clutches of the Inner Circle, sprint* across the Outer Circle, and make your exit crisply and cleanly.*

Simple, eh?

If this roundabout game seems too rough for you, don't despair. There are ways to simplify the task. I suggest you try one or both of the tactics briefly outlined below.

Go into the Inner Circle and stay there — In other words, go into stationary orbit and keep cycling the roundabout until you find your opening or find your courage, whichever comes first.

The principal disadvantage of this stationary orbit ploy is that you may eventually get dizzy. As long as you keep up your speed, however, there is no particular hazard involved. In fact, there are certain practical advantages, detailed in the section on Pathfinding.

Mini-Roundabouts

 Begin reading here.

Mini-Roundabout

This is a *mini-roundabout*. It works about the same as a midi or maxi... just don't bump over the concrete hump in the middle. That privilege is reserved for tour buses to give the passengers an extra cheap thrill. This small sign warns you of a mini-roundabout ahead. And, by now, you're conditioned to watch for and obey the Deadly Dashes... aren't you?

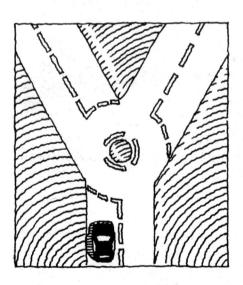

Gotcha!

One more thing before we move on to more advanced roundabouting...

In spite of my dire warnings about Deadly Dashes and other painted rattlesnakes lying in wait for you; in spite of advanced driver training which tells me to scan ahead, always ahead; and in spite of being caught out many times, I still get ambushed by a feature of roundabouts that is actually meant to make life easier.

I'm talking about a last-minute curl that is sometimes built into a roundabout approach. This curl is designed to reduce the radius of the turn and thus make it possible to enter the roundabout without slowing down too much. It works! But it also leads to problems for the unsuspecting...

- It produces a 'blind curve' from the approach road. You can't see the Deadly Dash, nor can you tell if someone is already stopped there waiting to enter the roundabout.

- At the Deadly Dash, the curl forces you to look much farther over your right shoulder than is common, comfortable, or convenient.

- When placed on a major road (as it usually is), the curled approach fails to give you all the visual cues you need to slow down adequately.

The end result can be an undignified rapid stop on your part when you get into the curl and suddenly realise that you have to stop... *right now!*

Consider yourself forewarned.

Roundabout Gotchas

⇐ *Please keep to the left!*

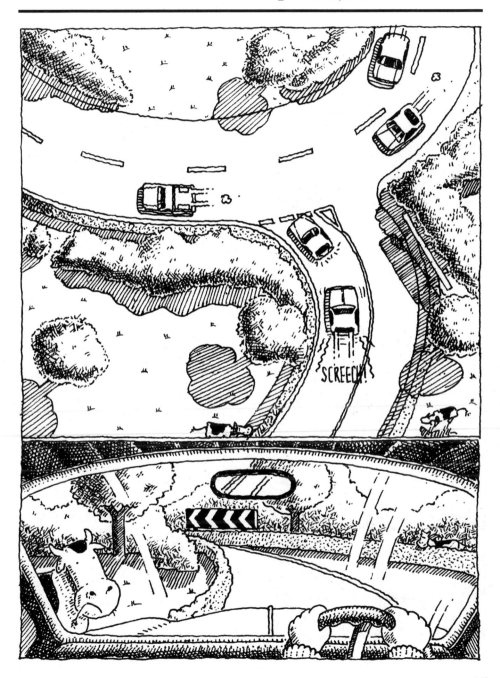

Begin reading here.

Sheep in wolf's clothing

All roundabouts work according to the principles just outlined. Really, they're simple (and kinda fun), but all roundabouts don't *look* simple. Here's a preview of some different varieties you may encounter.

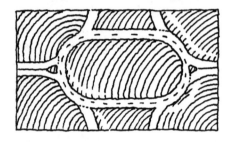

The only thing different here is the shape... no change in technique. You still Give Way at the Deadly Dash guarding the entrance(s), and you still signal when your exit is next.

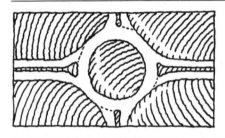

Same here... no change in technique. Give Way at the Deadly Dash, signal when your exit is next.

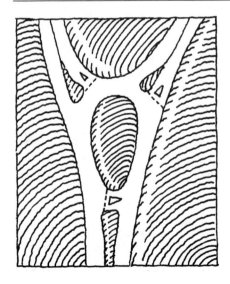

This is a rare case where some drivers in the roundabout are required to yield right-of-way to cars entering. Note the role played by the Deadly Dash in this foul treachery.

Double Jeopardy →

Believe it or not, there are roundabouts even more complex than this double doozy on the outskirts of Edinburgh.* But no matter how weird, the rules of *Give Way To The Right*, and *Obey The White Lines* will see you through.

Go ahead, try it out... where do you give way, and where do you not? What about going the other way?

* *If you really want to know, see note page 65.*

Complex Roundabouts

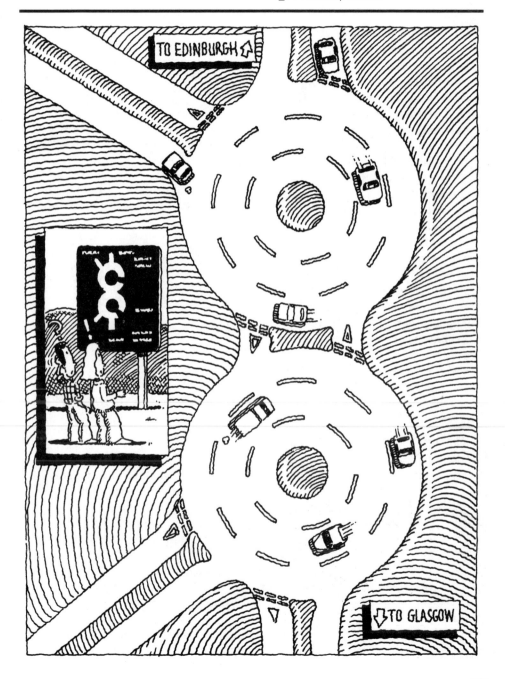

In molly-coddled and over-regulated North America many driving enthusiasts feel they have to bend the law to find the kind of excitement and challenge they seek behind the wheel. In Britain, you can generally find your thrills within the law, and aspiring to be an advanced roundabouter is a great leap forwards.

The true mark of the advanced roundabouter is the ability to achieve "pace with grace"— to take joy in executing that perilous crossing from the centre of the roundabout (the dreaded Inner Circle), across a lane of circulating traffic (the Outer Circle), and onto your turn-off road. To get full marks, you have to manage this traverse without getting rammed amidships by an Exocet missile trying to pass you on the left.

Two principles apply to this potentially dangerous conflict, one from animal behaviour, the second from military science...

1/ The Animal Behaviour Solution

When confronted by a vicious dog, never show fear or hesitancy. The same is true of vicious roundabouts. Thus, in making the dash from Inner Circle to exit, you must telegraph your intentions clearly...
Mirror check, signal, shoulder check, and go for it!

That way, other motorists will know exactly what you intend to do and, should you mess up, they can take appropriate tourist-avoidance counter-measures.

2/ The Military Solution

"The best defence is a good offence." I think that was General Patton's oft-quoted proverb, and it's certainly true when it comes to roundabouts.

If you play Nervous Nellie and creep timidly around the circle, you're going to have a bad time of it because everyone will be passing you. You'll become cannon fodder for the Exocets and, before you can mix a metaphor, your blood pressure is going to shoot sky high.

Much better to screw your courage to the sticking point and attack the roundabout with the same speed and *panache* as the natives. That doesn't mean barging in with all guns blazing, rather it means manoeuvring deftly with all brain circuits active and senses on full alert.

In Summary...

- Know what you are going to do.

- Make sure others know what you are going to do.

- When you do it, do it decisively, and do it briskly. Nothing you do should cause people on the roundabout to slow down.

Master the roundabout, and your self-esteem will abound. You'll be able to concentrate on touring, rather than driving, because you'll have overcome the major challenge facing tourists on British roads. If you really want the inside story, I suggest you write for a copy of **Road Craft**, this is the British police driver's manual. ⑦

Advanced Roundabouting

The Party Line

Official dogma in roundabouts requires you to flaunt the laws of physics. To execute a simple left turn, whilst staying within the lane markings established by Officialdom, you must make three separate turning movements (left, right, and left again as shown in the drawing).

These steering reversals are quite necessary if you are sharing the roundabout with other traffic. When executed with vigour, however, following The Party Line throws you uncomfortably from side to side so that Tee-Cee's charming head may begin to wobble like one of those little plastic dogs that people of questionable taste put on the back shelf.

IF TRAFFIC PERMITS, therefore, follow The Comfort Line instead.

The Comfort Line

There is no magic about the lane markings in roundabouts (in fact, some roundabouts don't even *have* lane markings!). So, AS LONG AS THE ROUNDABOUT IS CLEAR OF TRAFFIC, make your turn in a gentle arc, as shown. You'll find this line much more comfortable than The Party Line — *and* you can do it faster.

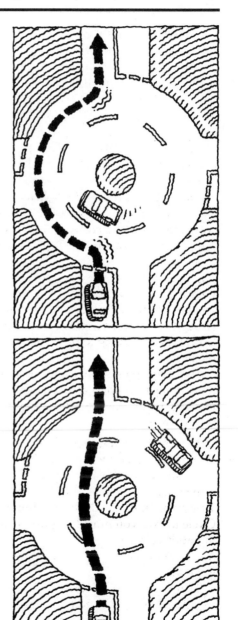

Country Roads

Begin reading here.

In rural areas the official speed limit is 60 mph (or as otherwise posted). The speed limit may be clearly posted for you to see, or it may be encoded as a white circle with a diagonal black stripe. This sign means *National speed limit applies*. In plain English, "don't exceed 60 mph." On most country roads the bends, bumps, and bucolic beauty will make that speed not just sufficient, but highly entertaining.

There is, however, one critical difference between posted speed limits in Britain compared to North America. In America, at least in *my* part of North America, a posted speed limit can be taken as a promise that the road is safely negotiable at the legal limit. Any bends or hills that require slowing down will be scrupulously marked and posted with an advisory speed. This is emphatically not so in Britain!

Without warning, you will encounter hills, bends, and constrictions that not even Jackie Stewart could negotiate at the legal limit. You are on your own to make appropriate adjustments.

Correctness and precision are critical on British country lanes because, typically, they do not have shoulders to absorb your errors. Indeed, they often feature curbs and stone walls to discourage sloppiness on your part. Other hazards include sheep, pony-trekkers, farm wagons, bobbies on bicycles, and frog crossings.

Cutting Corners

You can, if you wish, follow The Party Line on country roads and stay strictly within the lanes marked out for you by a benevolent bureaucracy. Or, where their benevolence has unaccountably failed, you can drive where you imagine the lanes *would* be marked if in fact they were, which often they aren't. Such behaviour, however, can lead to the dreaded Nodding Dog Syndrome.

You may find it more comfortable and efficient to cut corners... to straighten out the road by following The Comfort Line instead of The Party Line.

This can only be done on roads with little traffic. Also, you must never outdrive your eyes. If you're going to occupy the on-coming lane, even for an instant, you must have sufficient sight-line and awareness to be well clear of the lane before anyone else needs it.

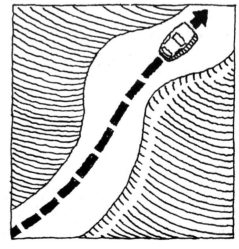

Urban Roads

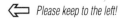
In built-up areas the nominal

speed limit is 30 mph. In big cities and market towns traffic may move a lot faster than the limit, and so , too, should you... up to a point. If you don't go with the flow, you'll create a hazard (and you'll feel distinctly harassed), but don't get carried away with enthusiasm. There will be plenty of unfamiliar things and hazards demanding your attention, so it behooves you to be a little conservative.

Great Expectations

I don't know about you, but I always expect roads to evince a certain rationality and consistency. For example, if I'm on a two-lane road leading through a village, I expect my lane to carry me in safety out the other side. At home, this expectation is almost always valid.

In Britain, however, if some-one's favourite pub just happens to have been built somewhat off kilter a few centuries ago and, today, it just happens to stick out into the main road by three or five feet, then so be it! Thus, you may think, "*Ah, I see this building sticks out into the road. But surely THEY wouldn't allow this to happen unless there was still room for two cars to pass.*"

Oh, yes THEY would! The road will either jog sharply around it; or it (the road) will suddenly cease to be two lanes wide. THEY also permit cars to park where so doing restricts the travelled road to less than two lanes.

The moral is this... don't depend on expectations of reasonableness in the design of roads through towns, depend only on your own good judgement. Thus, in towns and villages:

- Be prepared to slow down.

- Be prepared to jog around pubs, churches, parked cars, delivery vans, brewer's drays, fruit barrows, and assorted ancient monuments.

- Be prepared to stop if necessary.

- Be prepared to play "After you, Old Chap!" with on-coming traffic.

Motorways

Begin reading here.

Motorway Manners

Conscientious adherents of the Double Nickel theory of energy conservation and traffic safety are in for a rude shock in Britain. The official speed limit on motorways is 70 mph, but the unofficial limit is somewhat closer to Warp Nine.

I don't mean to suggest you can speed with impunity... you can't... but at least the speed limit is realistic, and should you choose to partake of some express driving, you will be in distinguished company. Oh, you may be fined (many are), but if you commit your transgressions with competence and common sense, at least no-one will try to stick you with the phony moral burden that is laid upon people who speed in North America.

It will further please you to know that "Traffic Vigilantes" are not welcome in Britain. You know the type... the ones who wear Woodrow Wilson-style gold rim glasses, breathe through their teeth, and try to enforce their own notion of a safe speed by cluttering the fast lanes of America.

No, the Brits are more broad-minded than that... those who want to drive slow keep out of the way and leave the zoomers to their fate.

A Little Discipline, Please

If you poke along the M4 in stately procession at 55 mph, be prepared for exile to the slow lane (the one furthest to the left) where you will enjoy the company of ancient Austins pulling chicklet-shaped *caravans* (house trailers) and hundreds of noisy, smoke-belching, evil-smelling diesel *lorries*.

You see, unlike us rambunctious colonials, the British still practice lane discipline. Under this regime, slow traffic stays in the slow lane and leaves the fast lane free for the zoomers. You had better do that too if you don't want a Jaguar up your jumper.

Oh, yes, don't clutter the middle lane either. Use it to pass slowpokes, by all means, but don't claim it permanently as a middle-of-the-road compromise between life in the fast lane and boredom worse than death in the slow lane.

Getting Up To Speed

One other significant difference you'll notice about British motorways is that the *slip roads* (entrance ramps) are very, very short. To get up to speed and merge smoothly with the flow of traffic you really have to move it... imagine you're a chicken with Colonel Sanders on your tail and you'll have some notion of the urgency required.

You'll also, perhaps, understand why I recommend against anæmic automatic transmission cars. If you *do* get an automatic, make sure it has enough oomph to get you onto the motorway safely.

Motorways

Exit, Stage Left

One abomination of North American freeway design has, unfortunately, infected British motorways as well. I refer to that hateful invention, the compulsory exit lane.

You know... you're driving along minding your own business when the lane you've found quite comfy for several miles suddenly and unreasonably becomes an exit ramp, inexorably shunting you off the highway should you fail to notice in time, or forcing you to make a lane change under pressure if you do happen to notice.

All I can recommend is eternal vigilance and perhaps an angry letter to your Member of Parliament or Congressman.

However, the British do help you out at night. The roads are a-sparkle with *cats' eyes* (reflectors) embedded in the roadway at strategic locations. The colour of the cat's eyes is significant, and can tip you off when you are in a compulsory exit lane.

Thus, if you notice the cats' eyes on your left have become red and those on your right are green, greenish-white, or white, you are to understand that you're about to leave the motorway.

If that's not your wish, signal, then move right (away from the red eyes), cross over the green(ish) eyes, and briskly join traffic in the next lane.

Keep up your speed, and check your mirrors. That should put you safely in a stream of through traffic until the next gratuitous ambush.

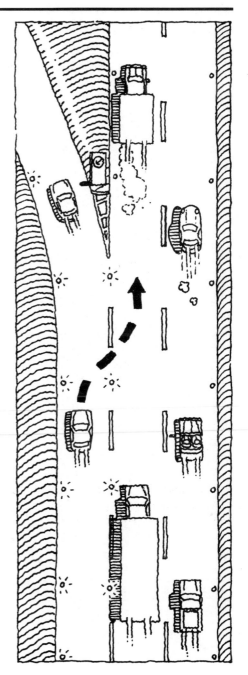

Passing Protocol

The British will pass one another under circumstances that would turn a California beach bum pale. However, one thing British tolerance does *not* encompass is passing on the inside. This degenerate practice is strictly forbidden. DO NOT DO IT! Especially don't do it on motorways. It is considered a much more serious offence than speeding... perhaps even more serious than failing to dress for dinner.

The taboo against *overtaking* on the inside applies equally on all roads at all times. Only two conditions excuse the practice...

- when caught in slow-moving traffic congestion, and
- when passing someone who is turning off (to the right).

The British, being masters of the Queen's English, naturally describe the situation in other terms... The driver's side of the car is termed the *nearside*. The side opposite the driver is called the *offside*. Thus, you must never overtake a *bloke* (or a *bird*) on their offside... they find it very off-putting!

Making a Pass

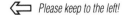 *Please keep to the left!*

Single Track Roads

In North America, back roads are usually gravel. In contrast, British back roads are almost always paved; however, they are often only one lane wide. That's not one lane for each direction, that's one lane, period. You'll find these single track roads most often on the high moors, the dales and fenlands, and in the Highlands.

So what happens if you meet someone coming the other way? Well, look closely, and you'll spy occasional wide spots in the road. These are called *Passing Places* or *Lay-bys* and they work like this...

When two vehicles meet, the one closest to a passing place is supposed to *draw in*, even if it means backing up. You can minimise stressful confrontations and time spent *reversing* by following advanced driving practice and looking way, way ahead. If you see someone coming and you are near a passing place, pull in and wait until the coast is clear.

Some exceptions to this protocol:

- On a steep grade, the one going uphill has right-of-way.

- If one of you is pulling a *caravan* (house trailer), the one who isn't had better *reverse* (back up).

- If you encounter a humungous *lorry* or farm machine, be gracious and back up.

- Sheep, horses, and other quadrapeds generally assume they have right-of-way. Be wary, slow, and gentle as you ease your way by.

By the way, if you encounter a sheep grid, don't assume it's wide enough to drive through... you may have to bend your mirrors flat to squeeze through.

An Heir-raising Tale

They don't actually "pass" in Britain, they *overtake*... sometimes under circumstances that make a North American shudder. Consider this scenario...

You are proceeding west on a two-lane road not far from Windsor Castle. Although there is only one lane in each direction, the road is rather comfortably wide... at least Tee-Cee's elbow is not carving a niche in the hedgerows as you go by.

Up ahead, there is a stately Daimler Princess approaching from the opposite direction and you are admiring its deep red colour and gleaming chrome grille. Then, to your horror, a white Rover pulls out to pass the Daimler.

"My God!", you cry, "Doesn't he see us?"

He does. He just doesn't care. The Rover's not suicidal, though. He knows the road is wide enough for three cars, even if the guy who painted the white lines didn't.

The thing for you to do is not to panic. If, in spite of your astonishment, you concur with Rover's assessment that the road is indeed wide enough for three cars to pass abreast, don't even slow down. Just move over a smidge.

This sort of passing behaviour isn't quite legal, nor is it condoned by most of the driving populace. But it does happen, and when it does it provokes nothing like the amount of outrage such goings-on would cause back home in America.

As the Rover flashes by and you move back to the centre of your lane, you notice the dignified matronly lady driving the Daimler is not the least bit ruffled by the preceding events. She catches you watching and gives you a faint smile and a funny little wave. "Hey," cries Tee-Cee, "isn't that...?"

Could be.

Take the high road

The British have a proverb... "If the road is straight, it must be Roman." But the eagles of Rome flew home a long time ago and sometime in the glorious history of this green and sceptr'd isle they forgot that a straight line is the shortest distance between two points. That lapse of cultural memory is manifest in a complex dendritic road network that more than somewhat resembles a close-up of Sir John Falstaff's eyeballs on a Sunday morning.

The myriad quirky roads are an endless delight to the laid-back rambler... and a source of endless frustration to the goal-oriented, hyped-up, gotta-get-there-by-6:00 species of North American tourist.

If you want to make time, plan on using the motorways (the M6 should satisfy anyone's lust for speed!). Otherwise, just accept the fact that it's going to take you twice as long to get anywhere as it would back home.

Before the Romans came to Rye
Or off to Severn strode,
The rolling English drunkard
Made the rolling English road.

... G.K. Chesterton

Free Maps

Most car hire firms will tell you how to escape the airport grounds. They may even give you a street map which might be just good enough to help you find the nearest Holiday Inn. But, given the complexity of the British road network, most of these give-away maps are functionally equivalent to eating soup with a fork... you only get the big noodles.

Somewhat better maps are available from your local British Tourist Authority (BTA) office.[8] There may be a token charge for maps *per se*, but you can avoid even that by asking for several of the regional guides that BTA happily gives away. These contain excellent little maps, along with useful info on tourist services, festivals, etc.

Whatever info you need about your coming trip to Britain, ask the BTA. They'll do their best to come up with the goods for you.

Treasure-Maps

If you want to do some advance route planning and perhaps nurture a glimmer of familiarity with British geography before you leave home, go to your local quality book store. They will carry (or can order for you) travel maps from publishers such as Bartholomew, Rand-McNally, and Michelin.

These maps are reasonably detailed, but not always so reasonably priced (in my opinion). Still, you can have hours of fun planning and anticipating your holiday so you'll likely get your money's worth.

Francly, my Dear...

Most veteran travellers know the *Michelin Guides* — they are the standard reference for most of the civilised world. The famous red covers contain detailed maps, authoritative restaurant ratings, lists of hotels, etc... in brief, enough micro-information to please even a tax auditor. At the risk of making a bad pun, Michelin will never steer you wrong.

I'm sure it's my fault, not theirs, but I've never been able to warm up to the Michelin Guides... too detailed... too clinical somehow... no sense of adventure. They're too much like that other French invention — the metric system.

But don't let me put you off. If you're one who prefers predictability over serendipity they might suit you perfectly. You'll find Michelin Guides in your aforementioned local quality book store.

AA, eh?

Most British people use the map books issued by the AA (Automobile Association). You see, almost everyone belongs to the AA, and while you may suspect this merely confirms the unhappy reputation of British cars, it's really a manifestation of the seriousness with which Britons view driving.

AA map books reflect this concern for detail and precision... some are as thick as a Bible and almost as highly regarded. Every road and cowpath in Britain is contained within the covers of an AA book in beautiful, easy-to-read colour with street maps of every

town big enough to have a public convenience. I saw one fitted out with a combination bookmark and Fresnel magnifier. Hitler would have traded a whole Panzer division for such a book.

For the casual tourist, some of the AA books may be overkill... but whatever you need the AA will have it!

One of my favourites is a volume called *The AA Illustrated Touring Atlas of Britain* which has more gorgeous pictures than the Tate Gallery plus fascinating write-ups of each region in the British Isles. The Touring Atlas is armchair travelling at its best... it can really help you through a long, hard winter.

There are many, many tourist books published by the AA. They are outstanding in their quality and range of interest, and if your local bookseller doesn't carry these treasured volumes, he's missing the boat. Write the North American distributors [9] for a free catalogue to show your dealer what he's depriving his customers of.*

Alternatively, you can wait and buy travel guides at the AA shop to be found in most major British cities. (Auto enthusiasts please note... AA shops also sell nifty car gadgets!)

---

* *I know, never end a sentence with a preposition. But with due respect to the memory of dear Miss Pringle (English 101), I thought you would really rather not read "...that of which he is depriving his customers." That's a construction up with which you ought not have to put.*

Finding Your Way Around (and Around, and Around)

In addition to being your biggest driving challenge, roundabouts will be a significant navigation problem. They induce confusion by forcing you to turn left even if you really want to go right and they tend to mess up your sense of direction. On top of this, while coping with the roundabout you must try to remember that very complex advance direction sign that flashed briefly through your consciousness many long seconds ago. If Tee-Cee, your navigator, has a quick eye and a good map, your burden is considerably eased. But, even so, you may have to resort to trickery.

Trick #1 — Memorise several main towns on the way to your destination.

The big direction signs may or may not point the way to the major city you are aiming for. Often, the sign will be crowded with smaller nearby towns. Given enough time and map study, Tee-Cee will be able to say whether the road to Ecclefechan is a short cut or an adventure, but there isn't much time for reflection while rocketing towards the roundabout.

So, you and Tee-Cee should temporarily furnish your brain cells with the names of a few minor towns that lie just ahead in the direction you wish to go. That way, the direction sign will always have something for you.

Trick #2 — Count-off your turn.

Don't rattle around the roundabout saying to yourself: "I have to take the turn-off for Llanfair Caereinion."

Say instead: "The third turn-off is mine."

Roundabouts can put both driver and navigator under a lot of pressure and it's much easier to count to three than it is to scrutinize all the turn-off signs as you zip by doing umpteen-to-the-dozen. The number you assign to your turn-off also determines your roundabout strategy... if it's 1 or 2, just use the Outer Circle... if it's 3 or more, psych yourself up and get in position to use the dreaded Inner Circle.

Trick #3 — Exploit your back-ups.

A: Stay on the roundabout.

Just go round and round as many times as you need to consider the alternatives and plan your exit gracefully. The Inner Circle is best for a holding pattern, but don't lose your nerve and slow down. If you keep your cool and keep up your speed, only Tee-Cee and you will ever know that you did such a dizzy thing.

B: Confirm your choice.

If you have sober second thoughts about the turn-off you've just taken, don't despair. There's usually a distance sign shortly after the roundabout telling how far to the next few towns. Cross-check with your map to confirm that you're on the right road before you go too far astray.

Pathfinding

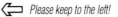

Asking Directions

Americans tend to be friendly and gregarious by nature so they will have no trouble asking the local citizens for directions... it's the natural thing to do and a good way to meet people. Americans may, however, find it difficult to understand some of the incredibly varied and inventively peculiar dialects.

In Britain, accents and vocabulary change radically from district to district, even from block to block within the same city. To prepare yourself I suggest you watch a lot of PBS.

For Canadians, the problem is different. We are more accustomed to peculiar British accents, but our psyche is dominated by cultural memories of isolation in a vast land. That spirit often whispers to us compellingly and makes us determined to find our own darn way through the wilderness, all by ourselves, thank you very much! As a result, we may tend to thrash aimlessly about the countryside until driven by darkness, desperation, and hunger to finally stop and seek local advice. Tee-Cee should take advantage of the stop to wrest control of the vehicle from Wrong-Way Corrigan.

For all North Americans my advice is the same. Please stop and ask. The British will be delighted to talk to you and help if they can. However, you ought to be aware of certain hazards pertaining to the Glasgow region...

Except for saying something favourable about an English football team, the fastest way to cause an uproar in Scotland is to walk into a pub and ask how to get somewhere. Upon uttering the fateful question you will become the centre of a smoky, beery-breathed, *mêlée* of Scots, all and each of whom will tell you in a rich, authoritative brogue a different way to get there. Your head swimming, you must try to sort out the contradictory instructions and historical precedents that fly about as they vociferate enthusiastically about The One True Way.

I can't explain this, I can only send you forewarned. Be aware, too, that the phenomenon is not limited to pubs and may occur in any group of two or more. My advice is this:

- If you must ask directions in a Scottish pub, order a half-pint first (see next chapter).

- Otherwise, seek out a solitary informant.

- Better still, ask a policeman or a taxi driver.

By the way, if someone tells you "Go down to The Cross and turn left," they're not telling you to look for a churchyard. In local parlance *The Cross* is simply the main intersection in town. Thus, one has Glagow Cross, Uddingston Cross, Parkhead Cross, *et cetera*. It's not always clear whether the intersection you are at is really a main intersection (and thus, *The Cross*), or simply an imposing confluence of minor roads pretending to be important. Perhaps the best way to tell is to look for at least one bank and one pub. See them? You are likely at *The Cross*.

If you drink at all, you're more likely to drink on holiday, especially since pubs are such a delightful and integral part of British culture (not to mention, a good place to find a cheap lunch!). That being the case, you should know that the British take a dim view of drinking and driving.

The legal limit is .08 (i.e., 80 milligrams of alcohol per 100 millilitres of blood). This is a lower legal limit than in some North American jurisdictions and it is vigorously enforced.

I don't wish to play Banquo's ghost and spoil your fun but, as drivers (and decent human beings), we ought to ensure that our indulgence does not bring harm to anyone else. The way to accomplish this is to know what we are doing behind the bar as well as behind the wheel. Hence, this chapter.

The Educated Drinker

The first thing you should know is that drinking and driving is really metaphorical Russian Roulette. They arrest people and throw them in *gaol* (jail) at .08 BAC (blood alcohol concentration) because driving at that level of impairment is equivalent to putting bullets in several of the chambers. But even a couple of "shots" can be enough to kill. My point is this... *Don't think that staying under the "legal limit" makes you a safe driver!* It doesn't.

The next thing you should know is that, in general terms, it doesn't matter what you drink. Whisky may be strong stuff, but beer is served in a larger glass. The net result is that you get about the same amount of pure alcohol from any standard serving of any standard tipple.

"So you see, Luv, WHAT you drink, doesn't matter as much as HOW MANY you drink."

Drinking & Driving

⇐ *Please keep to the left!*

The Common Sense Limit

Alcohol effects your ability to drive long before you reach the legal limit. In fact, any amount of alcohol impairs to some degree, but the first easily measurable effects don't occur until BAC reaches .05. At this point, symptoms of impairment are typically slight (some drowsiness and a modest drop in reaction time), so I've defined .05 BAC as a "Common Sense Limit". It's not as safe as not drinking at all, but it's a heck of a lot safer than being fully loaded at or near the legal limit.

To help you drink intelligently, I've provided charts for your guidance (overleaf). If you care about the quality of your driving, study the charts to determine how much someone of your weight and sex can drink without exceeding the Common Sense Limit.

The pharmacology of alcohol is not fully understood so the charts are really gross generalizations. They are accurate on average, but YOU are not average... you're a unique individual, and individual differences can significantly affect your level of impairment.

The charts don't account for factors such as fatigue or whether you've had a meal (reduces the peak of impairment but makes it last a bit longer).

Also, the charts portray a fairly short timeframe, equivalent to stopping for lunch or *tea* (the evening meal we call "supper"; *supper* is a late meal had about 8:30 p.m.). In other words, I'm not talking about long-term serious drinking here. If you're into that, forget driving, get a BritRail pass.

Real Men Don't...

Anti-booze propagandists will never tell you this, but some people really can "hold their liquor". As you can see by studying the charts, big people are especially good at drinking.

If you are large and muscular, you can drink more than a fat person of equal weight (and a lot more than a beanpole). You see, muscle tissue is well supplied with blood but fatty tissue isn't... the more muscle, the greater the blood volume to dilute the alcohol before it gets to your brain. Thus, the more muscle you have, the less you'll be impaired by a given amount of booze.

Real Women Do...

Women, on the other hand, are particularly sensitive to alcohol. Because they are (frequently) small in stature and (generally) non-athletic, they don't have the requisite bulk of muscle tissue to dilute the intoxicating alcohol. And, in addition to more obvious features, they have an extra layer of subcutaneous fat. This makes them wonderfully soft and cuddly, but it also gives them a higher percentage of body fat and thus a lower ability to absorb alcohol than men of equal weight.

Now you know why candy is dandy but liquor is quicker.

Note — *The information on alcohol presented herein is based on a variety of sources, including Transport Canada and the Addiction Research Foundation of Ontario. They have not, however, reviewed the material as presented.*

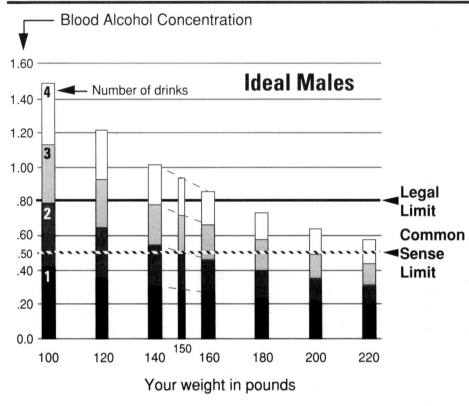

Blood Alcohol Concentration

Ideal Males

← Number of drinks

◄ Legal Limit

◄ Common Sense Limit

Your weight in pounds

How to read the charts

Find the bar corresponding to your weight (or interpolate between bars, as shown above). Each band of shading represents one drink, up to four drinks. Thus, if you are a male who weighs 150 lbs., <u>one</u> drink puts your BAC at about .30; <u>two</u> drinks puts you near the Common Sense Limit of .50 (better stop drinking); and <u>four</u> drinks puts you over the Legal Limit (better stop driving).

    The charts assume you spend half an hour per drink (four drinks would take two hours). The charts also assume you have an "ideal" body... not too fat, not too lean. If you're pudgy, or skinny for your size, your BAC will rise higher than the charts indicate, so err on the side of caution.

    Notice how the charts bear out the previously-stated observation that women get impaired faster compared to men of equal weight.

    You should also know that, in general, it takes the liver about one hour to metabolise three-quarters of the alcohol in a typical drink. Thus, "One drink an hour!" is a pretty good guideline to moderation for a civilised social evening.

How much can you drink?

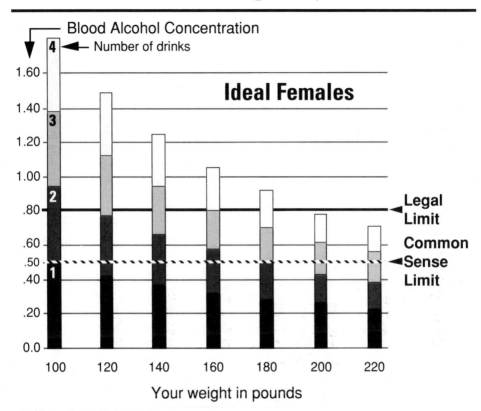

⇐ *Please keep to the left!*

Blood Alcohol Concentration
Number of drinks

Ideal Females

Legal Limit

Common Sense Limit

Your weight in pounds

Some myths about drinking

- *Exercise and dancing burns off the alcohol.*
  Not true. Nothing can speed up the liver's ability to metabolise alcohol.

- *Coffee can sober you up.*
  Not true. I repeat, nothing can speed up the liver. Time is the only remedy.

- *It helps to eat a meal before drinking.*
  Yes and No. Food in the stomach slows the entry of alcohol to the blood; thus, you become impaired more slowly. And, although the peak of your impairment may be less, the impairment will last longer.

- *"I can drive better after a drink."*
  No you can't. You may concentrate more, and that might seem to help, but even one drink causes your eyes to fixate inappropriately on objects which attract your attention, instead of scanning about the way the eyes of a good driver should.

Drinking Strategies

 Begin reading here.

Some philosophers maintain reality is just a dream. Somehow, though, solipsism seems particularly inappropriate behind the wheel, so if your reality involves some drinking and you don't want to lose your grip, here are some practical free lessons on how to drink…

- In pubs, order beer by the half-pint. Compared to ordering by the pint, this gives you twice as many chances to banter with the publican or serving wench* and only half as much alcohol to metabolise.

- Eat first if you're going to have more than two half-pints.

- At any drinking event lasting several hours, confine your drinking to the early part of the evening, then switch to soda water three hours before leaving. Consult the "How Much Can You Drink?" charts (pp. 54 & 55) to estimate your capacity and plan your strategy.

- In southwest England (Devon and the West Country), don't be fooled by the innocent-sounding local draught cider. It's powerful stuff! They call it *scrumpy* … possibly because of how you feel next morning.

- Ask the proprietor or your server to recommend a local brew. This won't help you stay sober, but it may prove interesting.

- In all but the most macho of pubs, you'll not be disgraced by ordering a *shandy*… a light, thirst-quenching mixture of beer and lemonade.

- In Scotland, *a wee dram* of malt whisky is an almost compulsory cultural experience, but don't be fooled by the Scots diminutive *wee*… drinks served in Scotland are bigger, and the beer is generally stronger, than standard English measures.

That means you'll reach your Common Sense Limit faster north of Hadrian's Wall. So, unless you're built like a sumo wrestler, be content with one wee dram only.

The locals will forgive your abstemiousness if you toast *"The king across the water!"* (Bonnie Prince Charlie) or *"To the confusion of the Sassenachs!"* (the English).

- In the Highlands, don't let it be known if your name is Campbell. Some Highland publicans have not yet forgiven the 17th century massacre of Glencoe and may refuse to serve a Campbell.

- If you plan to partake in one of the Elizabethan banquets staged for the merriment of tourists, don't let the comedy become a tragedy. It's all very well to play Falstaff for an evening, but one of you must stay firmly rooted in the 20th century reality of having to drive home safely. Tudor tipplers didn't have to worry… the horses always knew the way home. Stay sober, or take a taxi.

---

* *"Wench" is a once-honourable term that has acquired unsavoury connotations recently. Use only at Elizabethan establishments.*

Teatotal Touring

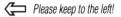

Where would Ronald eat?

It is, of course, possible to avoid pubs altogether. Even if you're not such an extremist, you will often wish to stop for coffee, lunch, personal comfort, *et cetera*. When the feeling strikes, you'll notice a definite dearth of fast-food emporia of the type we have at home.

Don't despair... the golden arches may be few and far between, but most pubs will happily serve coffee or soft drinks and there are lots of Tea Rooms offering delicious sandwiches and wonderful, extravagant confections dripping with Devonshire clotted cream (which is *so* rich it may actually be illegal in the Dominion of Canada!).

And don't overlook the old hotels in small towns. Even if they seem deserted, ding the bell on the counter. Like invoking spirits at a seance, the silvery notes will eventually summon someone from the mysterious nether regions of the ancient establishment. When they materialise, ask if they could serve coffee and *biscuits* (cookies) in the lounge. Usually, they will invite you to sit down and 10 minutes later will appear with a steaming silver pot and a plate of goodies.

As you sip and nibble, think about staying overnight. Though lacking the chrome-plated amenities of a Hilton or Holiday Inn, these old hotels abound in atmosphere, good food, and friendly personal service. Some are even relatively cheap!

---

* *One exception worth noting is the Westmoreland motorway café on the M6 heading north into Scotland. It's great, don't miss it!*

Eat! Drink! and Be Wary!

Regarding restaurants, I have three caveats to offer...

Caveat 1 — If you're looking for a meal, keep to regular hours. The British can be very fussy about serving times. Some restaurants even close for the staff to have lunch!

Caveat 2 — Motorway restaurants are generally pretty rotten.* If you have a perverse predilection for cold minestrone accompanied by 105-decibel Space Invader warbles, the worst of British motorway restaurants will put you in hoser heaven. If you would rather not re-live the café scene from *Star Wars*, get off the motorway and seek civilised sustenance in the small towns and villages.

Caveat 3 — Ordering coffee in Britain is not always a simple matter. Ask for coffee some places in Britain and they bring you horrible, hot, white stuff that is half coffee and half hot cream. They call it *white coffee*... I call it "Phillip's Espresso" because it tastes rather like coffee grounds and Milk of Magnesia.

To avoid this foul concoction, take care to ask for *black coffee* with milk or cream on the side. Actually, milk is a special order. You will invariably be served real cream. You may also be treated to real sugar for your coffee instead of White Death... delicious dark crystals that make a lovely tinkling sound as you stir the aromatic brew in your cup. Ah, a good cup of coffee truly nourishes the spirit! *N'est pas?*

Begin reading here.

Why Bed & Breakfast?

This book is about driving. It is not a general tourist guide about where to stay, how to get there, *et cetera*. But driving is more than just a way to get around. While driving, you are a participant in British culture, not merely an observer, and *Bed & Breakfast* is a part of that cultural experience closely related to auto touring. Besides, B&B is the most interesting, most adventurous, and most economical means of touring yet invented.

Usually, B&B involves staying in a private home. In return for as little as $30 or $40, you get a night's lodging and a big breakfast to start your day off right. Some hotels offer B&B as well, but usually the cost is higher and the adventure potential lower.

What kind of adventures? Well, that's up to you and the circumstances of fate (see next section).

Booking B&B

If you plan to stay at the Dorchester or the Savoy, book ahead through your travel agent. Except as a favour to you, however, an agent will normally book only expensive places because he/she gets a percentage of the total cost and the sum must be high enough to make it worthwhile and cover the cost of overseas communications. B&B is definitely not expensive, so this is one occasion where your agent can't help.

When it comes to B&B, however, being on your own is not really a problem. If you travel off-season, or make a habit of stopping early in the day, you can probably just take a chance on blundering across a good B&B, even in out-of-the-way places.

If you feel better knowing where you're going to spend the night, there are many guide books available to give you a run-down on price, location, and whether *the facilities* are private. Then you can phone ahead for reservations a day or two in advance. One of the best guidebooks is the *AA Guide To Guesthouses, Farmhouses And Inns In Britain* which catalogues more than 600 B&Bs.[9]

The much aforementioned magazine *In Britain* is also a good source of articles about, and *adverts* for B&Bs, country inns, stately homes, self-drive motor caravans, and other alternatives to conventional accommodation. Also, check out two fine anglophile magazines — *British Heritage* and *Realm*.[10]

Opinionated Guidebooks

Many authors with high standards and strong opinions have recorded their personal B&B and small hotel experiences in charming and informative guidebooks. The hostelry owners have *not* paid to be included (always a suspect practice), nor are such books blighted by a bureaucratically conceived necessity to be noncommittal or dogmatically even-handed. I owe a debt of gratitude to authors who have candidly and colourfully shared their opinions and so led me to wonderful out-of-the-way places full of character and history. Places to remember long after you've forgotten the cost. [11]

Bed & Breakfast

 *Please keep to the left!*

Cultural Quirks

Although many of our customs and traditions originated in Britain, there are still cultural differences that must be respected by North American tourists if the bed & breakfast experience is to be an entirely happy one. With this general caution, and depending on your goodwill and common sense, you'll do well. However, there are a few cultural quirks to be aware of...

A Drinking Problem — At home, we buy milk in 1-gallon jugs or 3-litre bags. In Britain, they usually buy it by the pint. That should give you some inkling of the expectations they have for consumption of this commodity. Try not to confirm the reputation of North Americans as being profligate milk-guzzlers. Be moderate in your quaffing of cow juice and ask your teenagers to try tea or coffee instead.

The Throne Room — Since you'll be staying in people's homes, and some of the homes will be hundreds of years old, you may encounter some bewildering sanitary conveniences. The British, you see, invented the flush toilet* and they've been improving on it ever since. As a result, there is an amazing variety of mechanisms for the traveller to master and some of them require instruction and practice.

To avoid possible embarrassment, I suggest you call a Privy Council meeting... i.e., ask your hostess for a demonstration of plumbing intricacies before, not after, uh, the event.

Cleanliness is Next to Gaudiness — A widely extant British prejudice holds that North Americans can't start the day without a shower (*Mea culpa!*). While they appreciate the personal cleanliness this implies, they are often aghast at the extravagance. Britons tend to worry about their hot water *rates* the way we might worry about a tax audit. Many homes are therefore equipped with miserly 5- or 10-gallon hot water tanks.

In the interests of avoiding a sudden chill and a scandalised hostess, make your showers short and sweet. If your room doesn't have private facilities, it's good policy to inform your hostess of your ablutionary plans in advance.

Finally, instead of a shower, consider taking a British bath... i.e., splash about in three inches of lukewarm water on the bottom of the tub and scrub yourself with a *flannel* (wash cloth).

Tub Safety — Be wary when stepping out of a British tub! Typically, the tub bottom is much higher above the floor than we are used to and the surprise of finding thin air where you expected solid footing can lead to a nasty spill. This is particularly a hazard for nearsighted people with short legs — and especially in Scotland where soft water makes soap even more slippery.

---

* *The flush toilet was invented by Thomas Crapper (honestly!!). One of the first installations was for the convenience of Her Majesty, Queen Victoria... hence, one surmises, the term "royal flush". In 1878, Victoria knighted Sir Thomas for his service to the realm.*

The Black Douglas

I remember old Mrs MacIntyre's B&B in the Highland city of Fort William... a cosy stone cottage in the shadow of Ben Nevis, a glowing fire at night. And 'round the fire a small group of tourists from Canada and Germany sat enthralled as Mrs Mac, in her sing-song Highland accent, told us tales of the old days when her husband was a *gillie* (gamekeeper) at the estate of the Laird, and she was a maid. It was like a real-life episode of **Upstairs, Downstairs** with oat cakes, tea and home-made marmalade thrown in.

She also told tales of The Black Douglas, who was the terror of the English during the 13th Century wars of Scottish independence. Mrs Mac's Christian soul prompted her to shake her fist and exclaim "He was a bad 'un, he was!" Just the same, frowning down from above the mantel was a portrait of none other than Douglas himself. On the same mantel were thank-you letters and post cards from former guests all over the world.

Room with a View

Bed and Breakfast accomodation is sometimes unconventional. Once, in Inverness, I was offered a converted garden shed. I was dog-tired, so I reluctantly agreed. To my surprise, it turned out to be rather pleasant.

I went to sleep with the sound of distant bagpipes keening on the breeze through a glorious red sunset, and I awoke to the singing of birds and the scent and colour of a country garden.

Serendipity-by-the-Sea

In the ancient village of Clovelly on the Devonshire coast, there are no cars... the streets are simply too steep and narrow for any contrivance more modern than a donkey (the original mode of transport). Imagine yourself arriving at Clovelly at the end of a long, hard day behind the wheel...

As you get out of the car, Tee-Cee thoughtfully points out you probably should have phoned ahead for reservations. True, but frankly you didn't know where you were going to end the day, did you?

As you hike down the cobbled, switch-back donkey trail that is the main route to the harbour (where the hotels are), you spy a lovely wrought iron gate leading to a sun-splashed courtyard of yellow and red roses.

Through an open door you spy a dark, cool passageway lined with oriental cabinets, swords and muskets. In the window, a gleaming brass sign discreetly offers "Bed & Breakfast". You exchange hopeful glances with Tee-Cee...

Five minutes later, Tee-Cee is relaxing on top of a fluffy eiderdown duvet in a pink and white room overlooking the sea while you (gallant spirit!) are hiking back up the hill to fetch the suitcases. When you return, weary, warm, and vaguely annoyed at your own nobleness (and the bulk of Tee-Cee's suitcase), your hostess is waiting for you with a hot *cuppa* and warm scones just out of the oven.

Welcome home!

B & B Adventures

⇐ *Please keep to the left!*

Adventure is an elusive quality. Sometimes, no matter how hard you try, everything will go smoothly. But that's what's special about driving in Britain... it guarantees challenge and adventure.

I hope that my sometimes flippant prose and Dan Hobbs' delightful drawings will help things to go smoothly for you in Britain, but not too smoothly. It's been my goal to replace confusion and uncertainty with a basic understanding of British motoring. If you feel competent behind the wheel, you and your travelling companion can concentrate on other cultural adventures.

For the driver, there is a special satisfaction and zest that comes from meeting the challenge of British traffic. This is derived from a constant internal dialogue that measures driving performance against our ideal of driving perfection. Some of the things I've told you will contribute, but for more information, check out the appendix, based on the teachings of John Powell... he will really give your internal dialogue something to talk about!

As for other adventures... well, that's up to you. All I can do is remind you that you are the master of your fate, the captain of your soul. My late father expressed it this way...

A Choice

There's no writing on the cross-road sign;
Its searching arms are bare.
Nothing at all to guide you...
You must put the writing there.

And each cross-road you come to,
Only you can choose
To take the right or wrong one...
For it's only you will lose.

...Robert Lockhart (1908-1975)

Epilogue

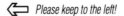 *Please keep to the left!*

① *In Britain* Magazine

In Britain Subscriptions
c/o Mercury Airfreight Int'l Ltd.
2323 Randolph Ave.
Avenel, N.J. 07001
    TEL: 1-800-783-4903 (U.S.)
    TEL: 1-800-521-7848 (Canada)

② *Many companies now offer all-inclusive quotes. Ask your travel agent, or look for such ads in Anglophile magazines.*

③ Exotic Cars

See your local Avis rep or speak to your travel agent. Other firms also rent exotic cars. For example, Wykehams:

④ Wykehams Sports Car Hire

6 Kendrick Place, Reece Mews
South Kensington
London SW7 3HF
    TEL: 011-44 - (0171) 589-6894
    FAX: 011-44 - (0171) 589-8886

⑤ Chauffeur Services:

Avis Chauffeur Drive
18 Petersham Mews,
London SW7 5NR
    TEL: 011-44 - (0171) 581-1023
    FAX: 011-44 - (0171) 823-8643

Europcar Chauffeur Drive
Davis House, Wilton Road
London SW1V 1JZ
    TEL: 011-44 - (0171) 834-6701
    FAX: 011-44 - (0171) 233-5193

U.K. Chauffeur Services
77 George Street, London W1H 5PL
    TEL: 011-44 - (0171) 834-6701
    FAX: 011-44 - (0171) 233-5193

⑥ Overseas Delivery

The following firms regularly advertise overseas delivery programmes featuring Saabs and Volvos.

Saab Export
77 Piccadilly *(Green Park tube sta.)*
London W1V 0AY
England, U.K.
    TEL: 011-44 - (0171) 491-4730
    FAX: 011-44 - (0171) 355-4267

Volvo Car UK,
Tourist & Diplomatic Sales
FREEPOST 30
Hatfield, Herts. AL9 7AR
England, U.K.
    Call collect from North America:
    011-44 - (1707) 26-2388

⑦ The Highway Code

The British Highway Code *and the advanced driving manual called* Road Craft *are available from:*

Her Majesty's Stationery Office
Book Shop *(Chancery Lane tube sta.)*
49 High Holborn
London WC1V 6HB
    TEL: 011-44 - (0171) 873-0011
    FAX: 011-44 - (0171) 831-1326

Regarding British phone numbers:

- *The 011 lets you direct dial overseas.*

- *The 44 is the country code for Britain.*

- *Omit the zero beginning British area codes when calling from North America — but it must be used when calling within Britain. Don't ask me to explain British phones... that's another book.*

Contact People

⇐ Please keep to the left!

⑧ British Tourist Authority Offices

◆ 111 Avenue Road (Suite 450)
Toronto, Ontario
Canada M5J 3J8
Tel: (416) 925-6326
1-888-847-4885
Fax: (416) 961-2175

◆ 551 5ᵗʰ Avenue (Suite 701)
New York, N.Y. 10176-0799
Tel: (212) 986-2200
1-800-462-2748
Fax: (416) 986-1188

◆ 625 North Michigan Ave. (Ste. 1510)
Chicago, Illinois 60611
Personal visits only.
Write or phone New York office.

⑨ AA Books

Order British Automobile Association books through your local bookstore, or contact the AA for a current catalogue:

AA Publishing
Norfolk House, Priestly Road
Basingstoke, Hampshire RG24 9NY

A good source in the U.S. is:

Britrail British Travel Bookshop
551 5ᵗʰ Avenue (Suite 701)
New York, NY 10176-0799
Tel: (212) 575-2667

⑩ *British Heritage* Magazine

British Heritage Subscriptions
P.O. Box 420581
Palm Coast, FL 32142-8985
or: Magazine Subscription Service
Box 244, Stn. LCD, Malton
Mississauga, ON L4T 9Z9

Realm Magazine

Realm is another great magazine for Anglophiles published bimonthly:

Realm - The British Connection
P.O. Box 215
Landisburg, PA 17040
Tel: 1-800-998-0807

Realm Subscriptions
3780 Peter Street
Windsor, Ontario N9C 9Z9
Tel: 1-800-998-0807

⑪ Opinionated Travel Guides

There are many, and the best are immediately apparent by their attitude... a sense of character and insight usually lacking in commercial guides and never evident in "official" guides.

Here's one I personally appreciate:

Karen Brown's England, Wales &
Scotland Charming Hotels and
Itineraries
ISBN 0-930328-43-4
Globe Pequot Press

The World Wide Web

See page 80 for a brief list of Internet sites that will help you plan your trip, and even book your accommodation or rental car.

Really Complex Roundabouts

There exist a few diabolical "Counterflow" roundabouts, way too scary for family reading. If you are the age of consent, drop me a line (address p. 79). I'll send complete details... free to the home of the brave.

Appendix

↙ Begin reading here.

About John Powell...

John Powell is a former racer, chief instructor of the Mosport Racing School, and manager of several successful racing teams, including Formula 2000 and Showroom Stock Enduro. Most of the recent winners at Indianapolis have taken training from John Powell.

John is also a consultant to government and industry on advanced driver training and he provides one-day and three-day courses in accident avoidance, emergency braking, and other aspects of vehicle control and safety.

In a way, it's appropriate that these teachings of John Powell be included in an appendix... he's been a pain in the side of the driving establishment for years. So much of what we are taught about driving is hogwash and John has had the courage, the analytical skills, and the proven track record to say so.

John defines "advanced driving" as doing ordinary things to a high level of skill. In a book, I cannot hope to lead you to this happy state in the same way that John could with intensive in-car training, but I trust this appendix will give you a better intellectual appreciation of the driving task and so contribute to your safety and enjoyment of driving, in Britain and at home.

John Powell may be reached at:

Powell Motorsports
Advanced Driving School
R.R.#1
Blackstock, Ontario
Canada L0B 1B0

(905) 986-2277 - voice
(905) 986-CARS - mnemonic
(905) 986-5470 - fax

Advanced Driving

Head Start

Anyone who seriously dabbles in sports will tell you the importance of getting "psyched up" for a big game. Ergonomic specialists have actually measured an increase in athletes' performance under the influence of cheers from the fans. The logical extension of this principle is for drivers to be their own cheering section.

When you get into a car, prepare your mind like an athlete psyching up for a competition. Behind the wheel, you are no longer an accountant, a housewife, or a civil servant... you are A DRIVER! So, stop worrying about the Mogul Conglomerate account, the kid's piano lessons, or the latest inanity of the Assistant Deputy Minister of Obfuscatory Regulations, and start thinking about the quality of your driving.

Ritual helps, so establish a few driving rituals such as:

- Do a quick vehicle check,

- Run through a brief cockpit drill,

- Fasten seat belts (and make Tee-Cee belt up too),

- Put on driving gloves, and

- Exercise the captain's prerogative to choose a radio station or tape prior to take-off (but don't play it 'til later, when fatigue begins to set in).

Be your own cheering section and olympic judging panel. Each time you tackle a turn, shift gears, spot trouble ahead, or execute a passing manoeuvre, mentally grade yourself on your driving performance. Say to yourself...

"Well done, Old Bean!", or

"Hmm, good turn, but my shifting was pretty sloppy.", or

"Cripes! What a klutz! I hope no-one noticed." (Fat chance!)

Of course, you can't really judge your performance meaningfully unless you know precisely what constitutes correct procedure. This appendix will give you the mental tools, an intellectual appreciation of the driving task to help you drive better than ever before, at home or in Britain.

Appendix

 Begin reading here.

The Seat of Power

In the teachings of John Powell, good driving depends on two main things: *How you sit.* and *Where you look.*

Good seating position is vitally important for a number of reasons...

- It affects where you look and how you use your eyes.

- It enables you to apply enough force for emergency braking.

- It reduces fatigue on long trips.

- It is important to your psyche (upright people are more alert than slouchers).

- It positions your seat belts correctly for best protection.

- It keeps you in control when things go wrong.

How to Sit Like an Expert

Most people adjust their seating position with reference to the steering wheel. That's wrong. Your first concern should be for the pedals...

Bring the seat forward 'til you can put your right foot flat on the floor beneath the brake pedal. In this position, your knee should be slightly bent and your backside still firmly wedged in the junction between the seat squab and the seat back. That's it! Lock the seat down and you are now sitting like a pro.

"What about the steering wheel?" you say.

Well, if you're of conventional anatomy and the people who designed your car did everything right, your arms will fall naturally into place once you adjust the seat for good pedal pushing. Ideally, you should be able to hold the wheel at 10:00 and 3:00 with your arms slightly bent. If you then put your hand on the top of the wheel, your arm should be almost straight.

If not, change the rake of the seat back to acquire a comfortable grasp of the wheel. If your car doesn't have adjustable seat rake (most British cars do) or an adjustable steering wheel (unlikely in a rental car), you'll just have to depend on good luck.

There are many reasons why proper seating position is so important (see above), but the main factors are ergonomic:

- Your limbs must be bent so that you can exert the strength required to handle your car in an emergency.

- Your motor control skills diminish drastically when your limbs are at full extension.

- The weaker you are due to build, age, or sex, the more you need to have your limbs bent when driving.

Advanced Driving

⬅ *Please keep to the left!*

The Eyes Have It!

The brain is a magnificent computer. Once programmed with correct information, all it needs is good data to get you safely from A to Z. But, like a computer: *Garbage in means garbage out!*

If your eyes and brain are occupied watching Wiggle and Giggle jiggle along the boulevard, your driving is obviously going to suffer. What isn't obvious is the effect of peripheral vision on your driving performance.

If you LOOK UP (far off, down the road), peripheral vision takes care of what's up close. To understand this, cast your mind back to when you were first learning to drive...

Remember how you used to line up a corner of the fender with the edge of the road? That was to keep you positioned in your lane. Now that you're experienced, you don't do that. You just look ahead and somehow, automatically, you steer right down the middle of your lane. That's because your brain's computer has learned to trust the information it gets from peripheral vision and it has relegated "lane positioning" to the status of a background function.

This leaves you free to scan the road ahead. Heck, you even have time to glance at your instruments and check your mirrors for trouble stalking you from behind.

Now that you understand how your eyes and brain work as a team, here's how to exploit that knowledge...

Watch where you're going, eh!

The basic operational principle is this: *Since you tend to steer where you are looking, you better look where you want to go.*

Home base for your eyes should be far away down the road. That doesn't mean your eyes should be glued to the horizon (in fact, they should be darting around) but your eyes should always return to the farthest point down the road, like a compass seeking North.

Dirt bikers know the best way to hit a big rock is to stare at it. Staring at an obstacle practically guarantees another "crash-and-burn" story. To avoid obstacles, bikers do this:

- Glance quickly at the hazard to establish it's location and danger.

- Then, avert your eyes. Scan for an escape route that goes safely around.

- When you find your safe path, stare at it and steer for it.

The technique works for drivers as well as bikers. Approaching any tight spot, such as a high-speed lane diversion, pick out the path you want and mentally lay down a dotted line to follow. Fix your eyes on this imaginary line and that's just where you'll go.

While threading the needle, you are allowed very brief glances at the hazards hurtling past your elbow but, DO NOT STARE AT THEM. If you do, you'll likely hit them.

This look-where-you-want-to-go technique works like magic on narrow British roads with hedgerows clipping one set of door handles and wobbly caravans threatening the other set.

Appendix

Begin reading here.

Cornering

Every year in the coastal waters of British Columbia there is held a very bizarre event — a boat race in which there are two qualifications:

1/ you must be a mayor, and

2/ your boat must be a bath tub.

Imagine, if you will, that Tee-Cee and you are competing in an even more bizarre automobile race...

- You must be driving a bath tub full of sudsy water, and

- contestants must all be naked.

Think for a moment... how would you drive to win a race like this without jeopardising your own modesty or that of the cherished Tee-Cee?

Very smoothly, right? Easy starts and gentle stops. But what about corner, how would you tackle them?

Perhaps you would guess the first thing to do is minimise the radius of the turn. Yes, we'll deal with that soon, but for now just think about that water sloshing around. If you rush into a turn and abruptly crank the wheel at the last moment, a wave of suds will go crashing out of the tub... *swoosh*, there goes your cover!

But suppose you went at the same speed but approached the curve differently. Suppose you cranked the steering wheel slightly before the entry to the turn... not much... hardly enough even to change the direction of the car... but just enough to shift the weight of the car and compress the springs a bit. You can feel the weight

shift — it's subtle, but you can feel it. So can the mass of sudsy tub water and it will begin to move smoothly to the outside of the curve, rising majestically up one side of the tub.

Now, when you reach the point in the curve where you really must seriously crank the wheel, you'll find that the water won't go splashing out. Why? ...because your slight advance turning motion transferred the weight gently and your bath was subject only to centrifugal force in the corner. By gently, and deliberately, inducing a weight transfer, you avoid a sudden and possibly catastrophic rush of momentum as the moving mass tries to respond to steering inputs.

The Pendulum of Weight Transfer

In a different metaphor, that sudden rush of momentum is known as "The Pendulum" of weight transfer and it's responsible for spilling things, for making passengers uncomfortable and, often, for making cars spin out on slippery roads.

If you, as a driver, wish to avoid all of these unpleasantries and protect your dignity, don't be a victim of The Pendulum... control it by understanding how to precipitate a weight transfer smoothly and gently before it becomes unmanageable. If you combine subtle early steering with smooth braking, you'll find you can take corners with greater speed, comfort, and safety.

Oh yes, you'll have more fun, too!

Advanced Driving

The Discipline

This is the litany drilled into students at the Powell Motorsport Racing School…

- Brake in a straight line.
- Downshift.
- Turn the wheel.
- Balance the throttle to the Clipping Point.
- At the Clipping Point, gently accelerate and unwind the wheel.

Brake in a straight line — Why? Because tires only have so much traction. If you are using most of that traction for stopping force, and you try to introduce a steering input as well, chances are your tires will suddenly run out of traction and you'll skid.

So, although in normal conditions you can get away with steering and braking at the same time, make braking in a straight line part of your driving ritual. That way, there'll be no nasty surprises if the road surface turns out to be more slippery than you imagined. You also get to feel smugly superior when you see the chap ahead of you go round a corner with his brake lights on.

Downshift — Do this near the end of your braking, prior to turning the wheel. Pick the gear that will match revs for the speed you intend to take the corner at. The gear should be low enough to provide adequate power and torque, but not so low as to cause engine braking.

Turn the wheel — Recalling our metaphoric bath-tub race, begin a very slight turn just at the end of your straight-line braking. Then, looking across the curve to the Clipping Point and beyond, gently dial in the correct amount of steering input.

Balance the throttle — You should neither accelerate nor drag the engine. On a short corner, don't press the gas at all. On a long sweeper, squeeze on some gas to keep up to speed and maintain a constant centrifugal force.

Clipping Point — The Clipping Point is the apex of the turn, the point where you begin to unwind the wheel. If you do everything well, your Clipping Point will be right where the "Comfort Line" touches the edge of the actual radius laid down by the road builders.

Gently Accelerate, Unwind — At the Clipping Point, you can begin to accelerate out of the corner as you unwind the wheel. Do not accelerate BEFORE the Clipping Point!

Sporting instincts and your white-knuckle passengers will both be appeased if you feed just enough throttle to maintain the centrifugal force already established on your way to the Clipping Point. With precise control on your part, timid riders won't even realise you have double-crossed them by actually picking up speed while still in a corner. A bit of extra acceleration coming out of the Clipping Point produces a very agreeable sensation of "squirting" out of the corner.

Appendix

 Begin reading here.

Braking

The weird bath-tub race metaphor evisioned in the section on cornering will help you improve your braking technique, too. With only a tub full of sloshing suds between you and public indignity you would always brake in good time and come to a smooth, jerk-free stop, wouldn't you? I think you get my drift. There are, however, a few fine points I'd like to pass along...

The Rolls Royce Stop

If you approach a red light with constant pressure on the brake pedal, the car will come to a gradual, controlled stop. The stop will not, however, be jerk-free... just as the car is about to stop rolling, the brakes will suddenly grip harder. *Voilà*, another nasty little nose-dipper! This is because the forces acting on a moving body tend to vary with the inverse square of acceleration. In plainer words, the slower you are going, the less force you need to stop.

Chauffeurs soon realise the practical application of this quirk of physics after being scolded a time or two for spilling *The Guv's* champagne. They learn to compensate by letting off on the brake as the braking force required diminishes approaching a full stop. So should you. Your passengers will think you a marvel of smooth driving.

Advanced Driving

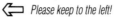

Threshold Braking

Theoretically, tires achieve maximum braking traction at 12.5% slip, that is, when the tires are turning 12.5% slower than the speed at which the car is passing over the surface. The practical upshot of this principle is that you must modulate the brake pedal to keep the tires at the "threshold" of skidding.

Only the most expert of drivers can come close to achieving the theoretical maximum braking performance using this technique. However, because we practice defensive driving and keep our eyes scanning far off down the road, we rarely need a truly maximum performance stop. Therefore, we can normally use threshold braking to stop quickly in most driving situations.

The more serious the threat, however, the more important it is to get on the brakes early and hard. Then, if the car starts to skid, there is room to modulate and ease off a bit. This is especially important if the rear wheels start to lock up because rear wheel skids are very unstable... that's why cars are designed to lock the front wheels first.

With an automatic transmission, modulating the brakes in tricky conditions is much easier if you shift to Neutral. You can do this only if the transmission is designed to permit quick slaps from Drive to Neutral. You shouldn't have to push a button to move from D to N, and there should be a détente to prevent accidentally engaging Reverse. If your car isn't properly designed in this way, get rid of it!

Deep Throat Braking

I hope the section on cornering convinced you that braking in a corner is not the *Done Thing*. Suppose, however, that you find yourself deep into a turn and it suddenly turns nasty... maybe you misjudged your speed, maybe it's a diminishing radius, or perhaps a sheep jumps out on the road... for whatever reason, you have to brake IN THE TURN, but it is not a life-or-death emergency.

The *problem* is this... If you get on the brakes too hard, the wheels will lock and/or skid. On the other hand, if you don't get on the brakes, you're going to go off the road.

The *solution* is this... Modulate your brakes... easy at first, but harder and harder as you rub off speed. The more speed you rub off, the more braking traction is available from the tires because less traction is required to make the car turn.

If on-coming traffic allows, you can increase the amount of braking force by reducing the amount of steering input. In other words, widen your turn and enter the opposing traffic lane. The hazards inherent in this are obvious, but sometimes even a slight excursion across the centreline will give you enough extra braking force to save a situation. It's better by far, however, to avoid the situation in the first place.

Anti-lock Braking

If you're lucky enough to have anti-lock brakes on your car, it is possible to brake in a turn. But possible doesn't make right... stay pure, don't do it!

Appendix

 Begin reading here.

Emergency Braking

On pages 72 and 73 are described aspects of conventional braking. Now let's look at emergency braking. The techniques described here are only for use in those situations that get your adrenalin pumping and perhaps leave you shaking a bit after it's all over. In plain words, these techniques are strictly for red-hot emergencies.

Lock-Steer-Release

If you lock the brakes in a turn, the car will skid straight ahead. If you then release the brakes while skidding, the car will dart in whatever direction the wheels are pointed.

If you don't habitually look and steer where you really want to go, you may be a victim of this phenomenon. Typically, the scenario goes like this...

• you skid unexpectedly;

• Panic stations! You wildly over-correct and countersteer;

• you look down at the steering wheel (everyone does);

• you release the brake; and

• off you go, into the bushes (or worse).

If you *do* look and steer where you really want to go, even while in a skid, you can actually exploit the skid to avoid an obstacle. The drill is this...

1. Hit the brake hard, lock up the wheels.

2. Turn the steering wheel a quarter-turn.

3. Release the brake.

The results of the drill are this...

1. The locked wheels will rub off a lot of speed.

2. Steering while the wheels are locked will not cause the car to turn, it will continue to skid straight ahead.

3. When you release the brake, the car will obediently and immediately go in the direction the wheels are pointed.

You can't do this successfully unless you remain calm and keep looking up, and away down the road where you want to go. Looking down amounts to an abdication of responsibility in a crisis, yet we are all prone to do this. Only by recognising this natural weakness can we train ourselves not to look down when things go wrong.

Advanced Driving

4-Wheel Lock (Braking In Extremis)
When all else fails... when it's life-or-death... then you can use this technique to obtain the shortest possible stop...

- Slam the brake pedal as hard as you can.

- Keep the pressure on until the car comes to a complete stop.

If you're driving a manual shift, stab the clutch pedal as you hammer the brakes, otherwise you may stall and lose the power assist on your brakes and steering.

With an automatic transmission, it's also a good idea to slap into Neutral as you stab the brake (assuming your car has a properly designed transmission that allows this). If you don't slap it in Neutral, the drive wheels continue to fight the brakes and urge you forward.

The idea is to lock all four wheels instantly. You don't have to be an expert, you just have to be brutal. Panic will help you find the strength. Hammer the brakes and you will waste no precious stopping time in trying to modulate.

With the wheels locked, *the car will travel straight ahead*! It cannot do anything else according to the laws of physics. The car may, however, slowly rotate on its polar axis. That's why you must keep the brakes on hard until the car comes to a complete stop. Releasing the brake before the car stops will cause the tires to suddenly regain steering action and the car may take off into the boonies.

If you execute a 4-wheel lock on bare pavement, chances are you'll flat-spot the tires and they'll have to be replaced... but that's better than trying to replace *you*, isn't it?

If you're lucky enough to live where it snows and freezes, you can practice 4-wheel lock and lock-steer-release on a frozen lake or snow-covered parking lot. Learn how to do it, then drive so you won't have to.

Anti-lock Emergency Braking
As previously mentioned, anti-lock brakes make it possible to brake and steer at the same time. The furiously active on-board controller adjusts braking force to each wheel to prevent a skid, and its pretty darned effective. Therefore, the recommended technique for emergency braking with anti-lock brakes is simply this...

Hit the brakes hard, and keep steering (and looking) where you want to go.

Don't push your luck by steering too much though. Even high-tech anti-lock brakes can't thwart the laws of physics.

Appendix

Begin reading here.

Shifting for Yourself

At the Hendon training academy, in suburban London, British policemen learn performance driving. One of the techniques taught trains finesse with clutch and throttle control... it's also a pretty good way for the uninitiated to cope with manual shifts and avoid those embarrassing "bucking horse" starts. The Hendon Start is simplicity itself... *Just put the car in gear and slowly let out the clutch!*

Notice, I said nothing about the gas, you don't need it until you are rolling.

To your probable amazement, almost any car will move off with dignity and decorum using the Hendon Start. Once rolling, slowly squeeze on some gas, and you're on your way to 2nd gear with satisfying lack of drama.

If the car stalls during your "Hendon Start" you're letting the clutch out too quickly. Practice 'til you get it right (should take about 5 minutes). The trick is to let the clutch out very slowly through the *take-up point* (where the clutch first begins to bite, the engine slows down slightly and the car strains forward a bit).

Pause slightly at the take-up point, then ease the pedal all the way out. As you do, the car will begin to roll. Once underway, promptly remove your left foot from the clutch pedal and put it back on the floor. Even if you goof the Hendon Start, the car will not heave and buck forwards... it can't because you're not giving it any gas.

Starting on Hills

Unhappily, the Hendon Start technique doesn't always work on steep uphill slopes. But if you practice it on level ground you'll be better prepared for demanding uphill starts (which cannot be avoided in Britain).

Starting on hills, here's what to do:

- As soon as you stop on a slope, pull on the handbrake.

- When traffic's clear, slowly let out the clutch until you can just feel the car straining forward against the handbrake.

- Now, simultaneously let off the handbrake, ease off the clutch, and gently press the accelerator.

If you misjudge the latter instruction and give it too much gas, grit your teeth and go with it. It's better for your ego (and a lot safer) to make a mild scene by squealing your tires than it is to chicken out and suddenly lift off... that's a certain recipe for embarrassing bucks and stalls that will leave you all hot and bothered in the middle of an intersection.

By the way, if you get to drive with any Brits, you'll notice they use the handbrake unashamedly on many occasions where North Americans simply wouldn't think of it. It's the *Done Thing* over there and probably a good practice to get into. And, because they use them, I'll bet the British aren't plagued by rusty, inoperative "emergency brake" cables the way we are.

Advanced Driving

← *Please keep to the left!*

Ritual Shifting

Ritual is important in advanced driving because it helps you to overlearn a task. That means you can do it automatically without thinking. If the rituals you practice are correct, they will look after you in a crisis and leave your brain free to attend to more important matters (such as thinking of a way out of the trouble you find yourself in). Here's the ritual on shifting...

Phase Shifting

Each shift between gears should have two distinct components:

1/ OUT (of whatever gear you're in).

2/ INTO (whatever gear you need).

In other words, don't stab at the lever like a karate master demolishing a plank. Instead, pause briefly in Neutral so shifting is a 2-phase motion.

Pausing in Neutral helps to avoid gear crunching. It also gives you a chance to play boy-racer by blipping the throttle slightly on downshifting to a lower gear. The blip helps you to match revs and ensures a smooth transition between gears, even when your downshift is a radical one designed to produce compression braking... though it is not generally recommended to save the brakes by wearing out the drivetrain.

Practice 2-phase shifting until you can snick easily between gears with satisfying little "ka-chunks".

Many cars are reluctant to shift into Reverse or 1st gear (Volkswagens are notorious!). You can overcome this annoying recalcitrance by either blipping the throttle as you shift (clutch pedal in, of course!) and/or by first putting the lever momentarily into 2nd gear. This tends to open the shift gates and usually works a treat.

The Ghost Pedal

Whether you realise it or not, a manual shift car has *four* pedals, not three. The 4th is the *dead pedal* provided to the left of the clutch on well-designed cars. This is the spot on the floor where you ought to rest your left foot between shifts. Your left foot should spring back to this spot between every shift as if your shoe were attached there by a strong elastic.

There are two good reasons for this:

1. It will keep you from riding the clutch.

2. Pressing your left foot against the *"dead pedal"* forces your back-side into the corner of the seat, thereby:

- allowing your seat belt to lie comfortably and safely across the massive bony structure of the pelvis below the Illiac Crest;

- enhancing lumbar support (and thus reducing fatigue);

- ensuring an upright posture (good for looking down the road);

- enabling you to apply maximum force for emergency braking; and

- bracing you to help maintain control in an emergency when people tend to get rattled about both mentally and physically.

77

Appendix

 Begin reading here.

Unparalled Parking

Just about every textbook tutorial on parallel parking tells you to pull up even with the car ahead of the empty spot you wish to park in. Well, the books are wrong! That's why almost everyone hates parallel parking and many people can't do it at all.

The secret is to pull up further than the car ahead. Then, twist around in your seat so that the corner of your bum is in the middle of the driver's seat. Now, look straight back down the centre of the car and you should have a good overall view of the situation you intend to back into.

With this broad picture, the magic of peripheral vision will work to guide you unerringly into your parallel parking spot with unparalled grace.

Please, Sir... I want more

⇐ *Please keep to the left!*

To obtain more copies...

Ask your bookseller, or write:

Driving in Britain
P.O. Box 405
Don Mills, Ontario
Canada M3C 2T2

Individual copies cost:

Retail prices, according to where you live, are detailed below. Books will be shipped via Canada Post, U.S. Post Office, or Royal Mail.

Canada

$12.95 per book + $2 per order for shipping and handling.

U.S.A.

$12.95 US per book + $2 per order for shipping and handling.

Britain

£6 per book + £1 per order for shipping and handling.

We welcome your personal cheque. Please make payable to *Rampant Lion*.

The shipping and handling charge applies only once per order... you pay just $2 (or £1) whether you order one book or five. That's our way of giving a discount for ordering in quantity.

Multiple copies cost:

Wholesale rates at very substantial discounts are available for persons, groups, or bookstores ordering by the dozen. For details write, fax or e-mail:

Rampant Lion Communications
P.O. Box 405
Don Mills, Ontario
Canada M3C 2T2

FAX: (416) 752-7482

The 'fax' number given above is also an answering machine. You can leave a voice message or be blamelessly rude and just push your fax SEND button.

E-MAIL: lockhart@astral.magic.ca

I wish I could be confident this e-mail address will remain unchanged, but you know how things are in the world of the internet... change is rapid and constant.

Few dull surfdoms

 Begin reading here.

The World Wide Web...

Fast becoming a major source of travel planning information, the extent of web resources is amazing, and growing each day. Unfortunately web sites tend to change daily as well and while these addresses are good at the time of writing, your experience may vary.

British Tourist Authority

http://www.bta.org.uk/

This is an excellent starting place, though like all official guides, it's a little stuffy. Why are bureaucrats so afraid to smile?

Rampant Scotland Index

http://scotland.rampant.com/

The BEST! Over 3,000 links to things Scottish. This site is a treasure trove of interesting, informative and useful information if Scotland is in your travel plans, or simply on your mind. Cool graphics, too... cute little animations that will make you laugh. There's a lively newsletter as well.

Automobile Association

http://www.theaa.co.uk/

Comprehensive and informative... typically AA. The site features an extensive travel planning section where you can pick a region of Britain and search for suitable accommodation, mostly hotels but some B&Bs too. Pack a lunch before you visit this site!

Pure Dead Glasgow

http://www.dis.strath.ac.uk/glasgow/

Pure Dead Brilliant! No cute cartoons, hardly any graphics at all, just tons of links to Glaswegiana.

Tourism Wales

http://www.tourism.wales.gov.uk/ wtw.html

Nice graphics, and lots of information, but much of it geared to tourist operators and potential investors. The cold dead hand of officialdom strikes again. Still, it's worth delving the gold from the dross at this site if you are going to Wales.

Northern Ireland Tourism

http://www.interknowledge.com/ northern-ireland/index.htm

Northern Ireland is on my life-list of places I must go, but haven't as yet. If it's the same for you, this is a good place to start. Though an 'official' site, this one has a bit of Irish twinkle in it's eye.

London sites

http://www.tourist.co.uk/

http://ukplus.co.uk/londonmall/

Both these sites are lively and full of good information about the city. Restaurant guides, what's on at the theatres, special events... it's all here. When a man is tired of London, he is tired of life — but to be tired IN London is much to be expected.